THE LAST FAITH

Karmak Bagisbayev

THE LAST FAITH

A BOOK BY AN ATHEIST BELIEVER

Translated from Russian by Joanna Dobson

ISBN: 1537271229
ISBN 13: 9781537271224
Library of Congress Control Number: 2016914251
CreateSpace Independent Publishing Platform
North Charleston, South Carolina

CONVERSATIONS BEFORE DAWN

"And I applied my heart to seek and to search out by wisdom all that is done under heaven.
It is an unhappy business that God has given to the children of man to be busy with."

Ecclesiastes

TABLE OF CONTENTS

The physicist Leo Szilard once announced to his friend
Hans Bethe that he was thinking of keeping a diary.
"I don't intend to publish. I am merely going to record
the facts for the information of God".
"Don't you think God knows the facts?", Bethe asked.
"Yes", said Szilard. "He knows the facts but He does not
know this version of the facts."

Hans Christian von Baeyer,
"Taming The Atom"

PROLOGUE

As early as I can remember I have wondered what people live for, what the purpose of living really is. In my earliest memories of childhood I had already begun to question why people are so afraid of dying and why they may suddenly stop being afraid and risk their own lives to save the lives of others.

In my youth, the questions that concerned me most were related to the irresistible attraction all life experiences towards the opposite sex. Why do some people, albeit rarely, make the conscious decision not to procreate? When, how and under what circumstances did the kind of human sex arise, which is free from the purpose of reproduction, a phenomenon that so sharply distinguishes man from animals, for whom sex exists solely as a reproductive act? Why such "free love", which was derided for millennia, common among some nations today and not among others?

Why do people get married and why do they get divorced?

Why it is that throughout the world, monogamous marriage has almost entirely replaced polygamous marriage? Why do married partners cheat on one another and why do they suffer jealousy?

Why do we consider some women (or men) beautiful and others less so? Why do parents bring up their children in one style rather than another?

Why is the difference in gender specific education gradually being erased today when traditionally men and women among many peoples and various social strata have always been taught differently?

Why is it that until recently an intolerant attitude towards homosexuality was prevalent, and why are same-sex marriages recognised today in certain Western countries?

Why is virginity in a bride no longer a requirement in a significant part of the world, whereas until as late as the middle of the last century, it was a widespread condition of marriage?

Why are experiments in human cloning banned and how long might this ban last?

Why are almost all religions opposed to suicide? Why is euthanasia still illegal, and why is policy beginning to change in a growing number of countries? Does suicide exist among animals?

Why do we have so many moral rules: do this, do that but don't do this and don't do that? Who invents the rules and why should I comply? Where does our morality originate, in God, or do we make it up ourselves? And if we do make it up ourselves, to what degree are we free to choose the morality by which we live our lives? How do our moral values change with time? And why has the rate of change so accelerated, that now, in the 21st century, a divide in moral expectations exists not just between father and child, but between older and younger brother. Why is society now adopting different moral values practically on a yearly basis? Why is the line between male and female behaviour so rapidly becoming blurred? Which laws determine the path of the evolution of morality?

Can a world without violence exist? If not, then when does man have a right to express violence and what type of violence is acceptable? What is the source of this right?

During times of revolution and war, why does a person who would otherwise feel an aversion to murder, become capable of killing without significantly damaging their sense of morality? Does man have a right of revolution?

Why is it that in the protest movements of the 21st century occurring in the United States, Europe, the Arab East, Asia, the Ukraine and Russia, we no longer see examples of undisputedly charismatic leaders, the type of which have appeared over several millennia at times of the world's most significant social movements? Why do we no longer see strong spiritual movements which are attractive and accessible enough to appeal to large segments of the general public? Why is the spiritual authority of all the world religions in such rapid decline?

How and when did patriotism emerge and why is it losing ground today, especially among the younger generation?

Collectivism emerged with man's very appearance on the planet and has over time played the same role for mankind as the herd instinct has played in the animal kingdom, namely, survival of the race or species. So why is it that since the Renaissance collectivism has gradually been slowing down the processes of change that initiate human development? Why is it, that as of the 20th century, collectivism has become a great source of evil and can generally be seen to be relinquishing its position ever more freely to individualism, particularly in the West. Why do we consider Western countries more "advanced" and by which criteria do we measure "advancement"?

What is Love? Why do we no longer hear about the kind of love shared by Romeo and Juliet, Tristan and Isolde, Layla and Majnun? Can this kind of love still exist today? If not, then why not?

People are born with very different intellectual, spiritual and physical abilities. So why do we insist that we are all equal? In what context are we equal and what is the source of our equality?

Why is man such a curious creature? Why has man experienced the urge to create ever since his appearance on Earth and why does he continue unremittingly to develop the sciences and the arts? What is a genius, a revolutionary, a criminal? What do these different types of people have in common? How are they different?

What is friendship and why does it occur?

Why are young adults so eager to leave home and achieve independence from their parents even if it means living at a lower level of material comfort?

Why did the colonial peoples living in relative prosperity, rise up and face a deadly struggle for independence in the middle of the last century? And why is it that despite the difficult economic conditions that followed independence, these peoples did not push to return to colony status?

Why, in spite of everything, is the world becoming more tolerant than it was in previous centuries? What is driving the shifting pattern of greater tolerance in the world?

Why do all nations strive for democracy despite fierce opposition from ruling regimes?

This was the endless stream of questions that besieged my mind: "why", "why", "why"...

The body of world classical literature gives the reader a deeper, finer understanding of the motivations for human actions, but no body of literature, neither the Torah, the Bible nor the Quran explains in a simple, accessible way, what drives people to act in one way rather than another...

Meanwhile, having received an education in physics and mathematics, I was amazed by the achievements of Albert Einstein, who at the beginning of the 20th century, managed to unify space, time, mass, energy, and later gravity. Einstein set forth his framework for a unified field theory, something with which physicists continue to wrestle today, and not without some success. In all fairness, prior to Einstein, other great minds had worked continually in an attempt to unify the knowledge that had accumulated in their day. For example, Isaac Newton succeeded in creating classical mechanics by combining his great laws of the fall of a ripe apple, the flight of an arrow, and the movement of the celestial bodies. J. von Mayer united what in his time had been thought to be independent concepts of mechanical and thermal energy, and set forth his hypothesis for the general law of conservation of energy. J. K. Maxwell brought together electricity and magnetism for the first time.

The various conservation laws of physics are essentially laws of unification and work to fully unify all the branches of physics continues to this day. The periodic table of chemical elements (D. Mendeleyev et al.) combined all contemporary knowledge on the chemical elements into a single table by studying their common stable properties. At the same time as Einstein, the Gottingen mathematicians headed by David Hilbert began a course of work which was to be completed half a century later by the French Bourbaki mathematicians. This group succeeded in unifying all the seemingly fragmented branches of mathematics on a single axiomatic basis.

When we consider a wide variety of objects endowed with a single given property (the axiom), we may derive all other possible properties (corollaries) possessed by those same objects. Further, considering a narrower part of the original set, possessing other additional properties (the axiom), we find new corollaries, true only of the subset. In other words, we find a subset with a richer range of properties than the original set. For example, defining a rectangle as a four-sided figure with four right angles (the axiom-definition), we may generate another property-corollary being that the diagonal of a rectangle is divided in half at the point of intersection. Further, considering in a set of rectangles a subset referred to as squares and possessing the additional property of all sides being equal in length (the axiom-definition), we may derive a new property-corollary, true only of this subset: the diagonals of a square are not only halved at the point of intersection, they are also mutually perpendicular. In this process, it is important to distinguish whether an assertion is the equivalent to another assertion, or whether it represents its corollary. For example, one may state that any property of a rectangle is true for a square but the inverse would not be true.

When one observes how scientific minds divide the objects they are studying into smaller parts, singling out primary factors and setting aside secondary factors, one thing becomes clear. It is easier to explore and understand a part than it is to study the whole. Sooner or later, however, one reaches a point at which it becomes extremely difficult for the mind to grasp a huge number of parts that have been examined independently.

However, this is also the most interesting stage of any scientific study because it is at this point that someone will notice a base property common to all the individual parts and succeed in bringing them together again in a single unified theory. Furthermore, at this stage, secondary factors can be taken into account which were previously discarded when focus was centred on determining the common properties of the objects under study, rather than the detail of their individual nature. Of this process one could say: "after the time to scatter stones, comes the time to gather them." In place of many laws, one new law can be written in such a way that all previous laws become a consequence of the new one.

What is the purpose of this process? Well, first and foremost, it is very beautiful! Aesthetics, though, are not the only reason for the scientific process of unification.

Unification basically makes material science simpler and clearer and, as a consequence, facilitates qualitative breakthroughs in epistemology, which in turn makes it possible to predict new objects and phenomena. For example, the prediction of the existence of previously unknown elements such as scandium, gallium and germanium was made using the periodic system of chemical elements. The existence of the planet Neptune was predicted on the basis of Newton's classical mechanics. In addition to the above, a new, more "basic" law helps define the limits to which any previous theory might be applicable and serves to explain any phenomena that exist beyond those limits. For example, Einstein's special theory of relativity explained the behaviour of bodies moving at very high speeds, close to the speed of light, whereas the general theory of relativity explained the curvature of light when passing near a massive celestial body. It predicted the existence of black holes and gravitational waves, phenomena for which Newtonian mechanics could provide no explanation.

The third benefit of the unification process in science concerns the problem of transmitting knowledge accumulated by humanity to future generations. Having consecutively passed through processes of accumulation, classification and theorisation, many sciences had amassed such a volume of knowledge by the turn of the 20th century that it would have been quite impossible to pass on that knowledge over a 4-5 year period of university education without creating basic general theories. It is not surprising that by this time the notion of the scientist-polymath had all but disappeared. Although the tendency towards generalisation arose with the very emergence of science, it was only in the 20th century that along with the other reasons mentioned above, it became an end in itself.

There is also a fourth reason why scientists search for the most basic, most fundamental laws of the natural world from which all others derive as a consequence. This reason is, in my opinion, the most important to those who devote themselves to the search and it lies in the following: When a man discovers the most basic laws of the Universe, he experiences an increasing intimacy, if not a full "interconnectedness" with the mystery of creation; he experiences his "God-likeness". The Bourbaki construction of mathematics on a single axiomatic basis was later termed the "bourbakisation" of mathematics. Russian physicist Y. Kulakov and his students brought about the "bourbakisation" of physics in the last quarter of the 20th century. The question is, is it possible to "burbakise" the behaviour of living matter, and especially human beings?

This book is an attempt to answer that question.

It is clear that living matter is also governed by the laws of Galileo, Newton and Einstein, but what makes it fundamentally distinguishable from inanimate matter?

Is the simple fact of the self-reproducing nature of living matter sufficient to explain all elements of its behaviour and the meaning of its existence?

And finally, human beings naturally conform to all her laws as an element of living matter, and yet they are still clearly distinguished by something else as well. The question is what? And is this "something else" capable of explaining human behaviour at the level of the individual as well as society?

Why has the individual en masse failed ever to observe (or perhaps been incapable of observing?) the Biblical commandments or indeed any other systematic paradigm? And it is important that we observe them?

Are they divine in nature? What "commandments" would God give to people if He or She[1] were to come down to Earth today? Religions undoubtedly proffer consolation to the suffering of the weak but they take their freedom in payment; it is no wonder that in all major religions man recognises himself as a "slave of God". Rather than limit the individual, is it possible for a "religion" ultimately to release the individual so that they become equal with God? What "commandments" does a person really live by and is it possible to formulate these commandments in such a way that man can actually fulfil them.

Does man really need God?

What is Good? And what is Evil? Is there a simple criterion by which one may distinguish Good from Evil?

Is there any true meaning to life?

In what direction is humanity developing? Is there a comprehensive law that governs the evolution of mankind?

Is it possible to give a clear, simple answer to all these questions?

It is, in fact, possible!

The book you are reading is neither scientific nor anti-scientific. And although it is written in the form of night-time conversations between the protagonist and God, it is meant to be neither theological nor atheistic. It is perhaps a first attempt to build a simple axiomatic model for the behaviour of living matter, including mankind, which may help us to explain, at least

---

1 It is generally accepted by theologians that God is beyond gender. However, it has been traditional to refer to God as 'He'. Quite reasonably feminist theologians have argued that it is equally correct to refer to God as 'She'. To avoid controversy some writers choose to use 'He or She'. For the sake of simplicity, in the text that follows God will be referred to as 'He'.

as an initial approximation, much of what is happening in the world around us.

Finally, what kind of specialised knowledge is required in order to read this book?

The answer: None!

Who is this book aimed at?

The answer: Everyone!

"If a man's brother dies and leaves a wife, but leaves no child, the man must take the widow and raise up offspring for his brother."

Moses (the Gospel of Mark)

PART I
THE LAW OF GENE PRESERVATION

CONVERSATION 1. THE LAW OF GENE PRESERVATION AND THE SELF-PRESERVATION INSTINCT: WHICH COMES FIRST?

"God, considering that You gave the law of self-preservation…"

"I did no such thing!"

"But, God, what do you mean? Man and in fact all living creatures fear death more than anything else in the world and are busy desperately struggling for survival!"

"Then why do trout swim to the upper reaches of a river to release their spawn only to die immediately afterwards, giving their flesh as food to help the baby fish survive?

Why does a swallow fly at the very tip of a fox's nose risking its own life to draw the predator further away from its nest of chicks? Similarly, why does a female wolf deliberately place herself within shooting distance of a hunter to draw the threat of danger away from the den where her cubs lie hidden?

In a fire or earthquake, why is it that people will do whatever it takes to carry their child to safety without hesitating for a moment and often sacrificing their own life in the process?

Why do male marsupial mice copulate so frantically on reaching adulthood, fertilising one female after another to the total abandonment of food and rest, only to die as a result of complete physical exhaustion? If the males did survive they would represent competition for the next generation in the battle for food over a limited area.

When female daddy long-legs produce hatchlings, they bring their own life to an end by offering their body to the offspring as their first food victim.

I can go on giving more examples if you like?"

"Thank you, Creator, that's enough. I see your point!

You gave a law according to which all living creatures, plant, animal and man, strive to procreate and protect their own kind.

And in producing offspring, in other words, in passing on their genes, the parents devote the rest of their lives to preserving them, providing food, protection and education aimed at enabling their offspring to adapt to their natural and social environment, until such time as they, in turn, can survive independently and procreate.

This is the real law, because it functions everywhere, always and without exception!

Let's call it the Law of Gene Preservation."

"You can call it whatever you like."

"Thank you. And, God, may I now add my own example which You might not have heard of yet?"

"Wise guy! Ok, fire away!"

"In 2012, scientists from the University of Minnesota showed, that more than a billion years ago, the first multicellular organisms on Earth, sacrificed their cells for the sake of procreation[2]. The same thing occurs in all organisms including the human body. There are cells which live exclusively to help the sperm and eggs transmit DNA to the offspring. Man lives for the same purpose as his cells."

---

2 Peggy Rinard. University of Minnesota biologists replicate key evolutionary step. *University of Minnesota*. [Internet] 17 January 2012. http://discover.umn.edu/news/science-technology/university-minnesota-biologists-replicate-key-evolutionary-step.

"And you are undoubtedly quite successful at it!"

"I am doing my best, God! It seems to me that in order to fulfil the Law of Gene Preservation, living matter will not only sacrifice itself willingly, as in the examples You gave, but will also rush to fulfil the law when it senses an external mortal threat. I can give You several examples."

"Let's hear your examples then. I'm listening."

"More than 7,000 years ago the Chinese noticed that when the marshlands drained and the land dried out, the wild rice growing in the marshes would begin to bear fruit and give many times more grain than usual just before the plants withered and died. In other words, 'sensing' a mortal threat, the rice was compelled to produce and scatter a maximum number of grain-fruits in order to fulfil the Law of Gene Preservation before dying!

The same thing happens with tuberculosis patients. It is a well-known fact that at the peak stage of illness the patient's libido increases dramatically.

The same thing happens to a person in the morning when they are suffering from a severe hangover, in the anticipation of death, as a certain poet once joked.

A similar phenomenon was observed among emaciated inmates dying in Nazi concentration camps during World War II."

"Yes, that's true."

"There are endless examples of this in nature.

In bee colonies, the male drones die immediately after intercourse. They leave their sexual organ in the queen's womb, in an attempt to stop other males from gaining access and leaving their own gene inside. In other words, even in the throes of death, the male protects his genes.

In other insect communities, such as grasshoppers and spiders, the female devours the male immediately after copulation which ensures that she receives enhanced nutrition essential for her to bear her offspring. You could say, that in giving of their flesh, the male contributes to the care of the future offspring.

I understand now, Lord. *The self-preservation instinct with which we began our conversation, is not a law. It represents a consequence of the Law of Gene Preservation. It is essential to the law's fulfilment and will yield to the Law of Gene Preservation, rather than come into conflict with it.* I used to think that animals could not commit suicide though."

"It is not suicide. It is self-sacrifice for one reason and with one purpose only, that it preserve its genes. It is a gene preservation instinct!"

"Now I understand, Lord, why when my mother had brought up her children, when they were old enough to stand on their own two feet, she said she was no longer afraid to die.

And Lord, I also understand why people say that there is no greater sorrow for any living being than to suffer the death of an offspring."

"Your understanding of the Law of Gene Preservation has begun to deepen."

"There is one more question though, that I'd like to ask you today, Lord. What made You give the Law of Gene Preservation to all living things?"

"Do you really think you would be standing here before me today if it was not for this law?"

"Sorry, that was a stupid question."

"Don't worry. Until tomorrow then."

"Until tomorrow? Thank you, God."

CONVERSATION 2. GENE PRESERVATION AND THE "BASIC" INSTINCT.

"God, is that You?"

"Of course. Do you have anything you would like to ask me today?"

"Yes. Today, God, I would like to ask you about what we call the sexual instinct, or the basic instinct, or even the instinct of procreation, which people believe You gave to all living beings as a law of nature."

"I don't know what you are talking about. What are you referring to?"

"For as long as anyone can remember people have been thinking about it, writing novels, painting pictures, producing films, carrying out heroic feats and great crimes all in the name of this instinct."

"And still and I do not understand what you are talking about."

"Well, according to this instinct, all living beings of the opposite sex, even including plants, are drawn to have intercourse with each other, as a result of which Your Law of Gene Preservation is realised. So, perhaps this means that the Sexual instinct is primary and the Law of Gene Preservation is secondary?"

"Now I see what you are getting at...

What you call the basic instinct is simply a means to realise the Law of Gene Preservation! Some of the simplest organisms and plants know nothing about the sexual instinct but that does not stop them from multiplying! There's cell division, vegetative propagation, budding, and so on.

As far as the basic or sexual instinct is concerned, it is simply a starting mechanism for the realisation of the Law of Gene Preservation.

Take animals for example! They only copulate at certain times in the year and purely for the sake of gene preservation. It is only man who has over time become more cunning about the matter. Nonetheless, even human beings get married eventually and apply their 'sexual instinct' directly with its true purpose of preserving their genes. You see?"

"Yes, thank you, I see now."

"What do you see?"

"I understand now that the basic instinct is not primary but simply serves as a trigger for the Law of Gene Preservation. It is its point of departure so to speak. The gene preservation instinct in parents actually works much longer, right up until the moment that the offspring are capable of independent survival and reproduction.

Now I can cite my own example to illustrate the supremacy of the Law of Gene Preservation over the basic instinct.

Zoologists have recounted the following case about the lives of wild animals. In a family of wild Indian tigers, a mother-tigress died, and the father-tiger took full responsibility for the upbringing of their two small cubs. At this time, a 'girlfriend' came to visit him, a tigress in heat from a neighbouring valley, who he had visited previously with the sole natural aim of mating. Sensing a possible threat to the cubs from the approaching guest, the father-tiger adopted a fighting stance and with a menacing roar drove the uninvited neighbour away, his whole appearance indicating that he was prepared to enter into a deadly battle for the sake of his offspring. It is only now, God, after your explanation that I fully understand the father-tiger's behaviour. He overcame his basic instinct for the sake of protecting his genes."

"You are picking up more quickly now. This is encouraging. Until tomorrow then."

"Wait, I have remembered another example, along the same lines from the life of African lions. It is a well-known fact that once a lion has driven away or killed the alpha male and taken over a pride, it will eat its predecessor's pups. This occurs when the mother-lioness is away hunting, otherwise she would engage the male lion in a deadly battle in order to save her cubs. When the lioness returns she sets about a sorrowful and futile search for her missing cubs. Afterwards, she will experience a sudden intense period of estruation and mate with her children's killer. Only now do I understand her behaviour which so shocked me when I originally heard this story. Once she is convinced that her cubs will never return she is ready to conceive again because she must preserve her genes. I can also understand the terrible cruelty of the lion-killer. In killing another male lion's cubs, it acts in the interests of preserving its own genes exclusively. That's all I wanted to add."

"That's a good example. Let's finish there for today."

"Ok, until tomorrow."

"Until tomorrow."

CONVERSATION 3. GENE PRESERVATION AND PRESERVATION OF THE SPECIES. WAR - REVOLUTION - PATRIOTISM - HEROISM

"Hello, God. Why do you always come so early, at dawn...?"

"Because that's when you wait for me."

"That's true. It is in these minutes before the first rays of the sun have appeared, and the stars are fading, one by one, and the sky is beginning to lose its blackness, that I feel a kind of inexplicable excitement, a burning and trembling all over my body. I think I have been waiting for You all my life..."

"What will we focus on today?"

"The species preservation instinct, God, which is thought to be no less fundamental than the Law of Gene Preservation! It is also called the herd instinct."

"Seriously? And what is it?"

"It is the idea that congregatory species and herd animals including humans, that is, members of the same species, will not eat each other and will come to each other's aid. For example, adult elephants will rescue calves in adversity even if they are not their own blood. Fighting buffaloes-males will enter into a deadly battle with a pride of lions, in an attempt to rescue the entire herd. Dolphins will work long and hard to save a weak, sick or injured relative constantly pushing them upwards to the surface of the water to prevent them from drowning. In other words, the instinct of conservation of the species is a common action for the preservation of the collective gene. That's all."

"Do you understand what you have just said? What is a 'collective gene'?

And what do you mean 'members of the same species do not eat each other'?

And what about the example you mentioned of the alpha male in a lion's pride, who came to power, and straight away ate the pups of the ousted leader, despite the fact that they shared a close genetic relationship? Cannibalism occurs in almost all predators when faced with extreme conditions of survival, including man. Herbivores, when faced with conditions of hunger, will take the last food from a weaker sibling, dooming it to death by starvation, to say nothing of what human beings are capable of.

Herd communities are unstable. They break up and will often fight to the death over food or territory with individuals who were members of the same herd just the day before. And wolves, for example, who regularly come together in packs will just as often break away to live alone or in pairs. Can you guess why animals come together in herds and why the herd breaks up or shall I tell you?"

"I'll have a go at it myself. It must be Your Law of Gene Preservation again, God.

People and animals come together in herd-communities with their own kind exclusively to a single end. Each individual strives to preserve their own genes but achieving that alone can become extremely difficult or even impossible.

It is easier to find a partner for the realisation of the basic instinct as a member of a herd and so, ultimately, the prime principle in play is still the Law of Gene Preservation. It is easier to defend oneself from a more powerful enemy as a member of a herd. A pack of hyenas, for example, can face down a powerful predator like a lion, whereas an individual hyena would have no chance. In a herd it is easier to hunt and gather large sources of food, which it would be impossible for a lone animal to find. This is the case for lions, wolves and all other herd predators, including mankind.

The unification of human beings into ever larger communities, beginning with tribes and clans in prehistoric times, then nations and states in the Middle Ages, continues today in the process called world globalisation. The reason for globalisation is the same as it was a thousand years ago. It provides the best conditions for preserving one's own gene.

However, the communal existence provided by the herd develops a code of collective behaviour among its members which is required for this type of coexistence to be possible, namely, mutual support and assistance, as we saw in the examples of the elephants and dolphins.

The human collective behavioural code has acquired a particularly complex form but despite all this, the species preservation instinct instantly disappears when it is no longer necessary or when it conflicts with the Law of Gene Preservation, which remains the dominant factor in any set of circumstances.

Usually, the entire herd serves to preserve the gene of the dominant family, helping to raise its offspring. But as soon as a non-dominant male tries to realise its own Law of Gene Preservation and approaches the harem of the dominant male, it will be immediately expelled from the herd or even killed by the dominant male, who fearing the intrusion of a foreign gene into his harem first and foremost perceives a threat to the preservation of its own gene. Young sexually mature males tend to drop out of the herd, exercising their own right to gene preservation. No herd can prevent them doing so, however strong their bonds.

Here you can see, that ***the Law of Gene Preservation is primary, and the species preservation instinct is secondary.***"

"I am glad that you understand the difference."

"I would like to point out though, that when the severity of external circumstances makes individual gene preservation impossible, the living organism will sacrifice itself in order to preserve other closely related genes. For example, in conditions of acute food shortage, the predatory bacterium Myxococcus Xanthus aggregate in the millions to form a 'fruiting body.' Only the bacteria positioned at the interior survive, the rest perish. Biologists call this 'natural altruism.'

We can see from this example that the Law of Gene Preservation can function purely as a species preservation instinct while remaining its principal cause, whereas the species preservation instinct would not exist at all if it was not for the gene preservation instinct.

Among human beings, the most striking acts of self-sacrifice for the sake of others become the stuff of legend and are remembered for centuries. Judging by its consequences, the most impressive act of self-sacrifice for the sake of others occurred almost two thousand years ago.

And it is with this story that I would like to move on to discuss the instinct of preservation of the species as it exists in the human society.

Often you hear people claiming that this instinct does not work in man because people are constantly fighting and killing each other. Now that I understand that the instinct for preservation of the species originates in the Law of Gene Preservation, I realise that this instinct actually works very well among people, it is just that our concept of species is neither static nor comprehensive. It is constantly changing according to circumstance. As a child taking part in street fights I knew for certain that my species were the other kids from my street because being together with them was the only way I would survive, i.e. realise the self-preservation instinct so that in the future I would still be able to fulfil the Law of Gene Preservation. Whilst growing up, a person goes from one species to another, which they either recognise as their own, or they do not, in which case they will try to separate themselves from it.

When an external aggressor attacks a person's homeland they join in a holy war so that together with their fellow countrymen they may save their right to gene preservation. At this point, a person's species is their country's entire population.

In this case, the race-preservation instinct is called Patriotism.

When the country's king and entourage or president and oligarchs rob their own people driving them into poverty and injustice, making it impossible for the individual to realise the right You have given them to gene preservation, then the people rise up in revolution. Now the species is a rebellious nation.

In this case, the instinct for preservation of the species is called Revolution.

The smallest, but the most reliable species a human being can belong to is the family."

"Ok, so tell me then, human being, can patriotism be reduced solely to a manifestation of the species preservation instinct, which, in your opinion is, in turn, an effect of the Law of Gene Preservation? What is the origin of Patriotism? On what is it based?"

"No, patriotism can't be reduced to the species preservation instinct. Patriotism begins with the most primitive living creatures, which mark their habitat and protect it fiercely in order to safeguard their existence, fulfil Your Law of Gene Preservation and pass the area on to their offspring. If the living creature is also a social being then patriotism centres not only on the protection of one's territory but the common battle together with one's herd or pack against external aggressors. Human patriotism also arose in historic times when no other contact existed between alien tribes other than mutual destruction. Patriotism represented a natural consequence of the collective striving for gene preservation."

"You have explained very clearly how patriotism emerged. What else is your human patriotism based on?"

"The foundations of patriotism were strengthened in the commonality of language, preferences for the same types of food and clothing, in developed tribal (and within the tribe, family) traditions and rituals, manners, and more specifically views on the manner and style of behaviour, in adaptation to a shared natural environment and climate, in communal song and dance, in shared culture and art forms and in the difference between this and the rest of the world. Yet the older generation, practically the world over, compare themselves with the younger generation and complain that young people are much less patriotic than they. Is this true? And if so, why?"

"Let's discuss that later when we look at the evolution of human society more fully. You are not ready for that yet."

"Ok, God, then I shall move on to the next theme. Now I understand, God, why we people love our heroes so much, why we compose songs and legends in their honour."

"And why is it?"

"Because in leading us into battle, being the first to launch an attack on the enemy, our heroes do for the rest of us what we cannot do alone; they head the collective defence of the right of every individual to gene preservation."

"Well, your thinking is generally valid. But are you certain that it is only the protection of the Law of Gene Preservation that motivates you, human beings, to participate in mortal combat, war and revolution? For example, it is mostly young people who take part in revolutions, those who have no children of their own and are still too young to think about having them. Could there perhaps be some other reason, so powerful that it motivates man to overcome the self-preservation instinct or even the Law of Gene Preservation?"

"It turns out that there is, but what is it, Creator?"

"Once again, we will talk about this later when we discover how human beings differ from the animal kingdom. We have talked enough for today. Look, it is light already.

See you tomorrow?"

"Yes, see you tomorrow!"

CONVERSATION 4. GENE PRESERVATION AND THE MATERNAL INSTINCT

"God, I have been delving through materials on various human instincts and I have found that the so-called maternal (or parental) instinct seems to coincide exactly with the Law of Gene Preservation. Can I assume that these are simply different names for the same thing?"

"Well, what do you understand by the maternal instinct?"

"The maternal instinct is the profound desire a woman (or human being in general) has to bear a child, for whom she will provide protection, nurture, instruction, affection and happiness."

"Is that all?"

"In principle, yes."

"Then how do you explain the well-known parable from the Old Testament (which is very well crafted by the way) about the woman who came to Solomon for judgement and was willing to give up her child to save it from being killed. She put aside everything that you have just described as the maternal instinct."

"I don't know...although wait! I think I've got it! She overcame the maternal instinct for the sake of gene preservation! The gene must be preserved at all costs!"

"Exactly! In some species, for example in sea turtles, the maternal instinct may be non-existent. They lay their eggs, bury them deep in the sand on a beach and then leave the nest forever. The sea turtle hatchlings make an immediate dash for the water, but on the way become victim to various predators. Rarely does a hatchling make it to the ocean alive."

"So how do sea turtles fulfil the Law of Gene Preservation which is essential to all living creatures?"

"It's quite simple! They lay up to one thousand eggs during the nesting period and so at least one turtle is bound to survive!"

"God, I'd like to return to our textbook example of the lions. After a pride takeover when the new alpha male kills his competitor's cubs, the mother-lioness comes into heat almost immediately despite having experienced deep maternal grief. The female is very quickly ready to mate and to conceive new cubs to replace the ones she has lost. So in this example, the Law of Gene Preservation prevails over the maternal instinct once again.

So, it turns out that *the maternal instinct does not exist independently. It is simply a consequence of the Law of Gene Preservation* and once again simply represents a means of either manifesting or exemplifying this law?"

"Well done! Not bad!"

"God, I've realised another thing too. Man is very clearly aware of all the human instincts related to the Law of Gene Preservation: self-preservation, the sexual instinct, the instinct to preserve the species and now the maternal instinct too. We respond to all these instincts for the sake of the Law of Gene Preservation and yet man, like all other living matter, neither understands nor feels this directly. Why is that?"

"You are quite right! Well, like all other living matter, there is no need for man to feel or be aware of the Law of Gene Preservation. It is only now that people have learned to cut corners and follow the basic instinct without getting as far as gene preservation, i.e. protecting themselves from the possibility of conception. Imagine if primitive humans had learned to be so cunning. Who knows whether you would have been standing here before me now or not."

"Oh, I don't know about that..."

"It's true! Animals cannot afford themselves the luxury. The basic instinct leads them straight to the Law of Gene Preservation! And nothing else besides!"

"So, God, why have you allowed human beings to do this? What is it aside from the Law of Gene Preservation that You have given man that distinguishes him so sharply from all other living matter?"

"Just one small feature, which we will discuss in detail later. This feature so changed man that even I was surprised."

"So, God, what is it?"

"Patience, my friend, patience!"

"God, I have another question. All the instincts we have explored (self-preservation, the sexual instinct, the instinct to preserve the species, and now the maternal instinct) are secondary to and originate from the Law of Gene Preservation under certain conditions. But it is not very convenient to have to start from the beginning, namely from the Law of Gene Preservation, every time we explain another phenomenon. It would be much quicker and far easier to refer to one or more of the consequences-instincts like mathematicians do, by proving a theorem, and then referring to the theorem or even a consequence of it, rather than referring every time to the basic axioms from which the theorem results. Is it ok with You if I follow this approach?"

"Of course. That is just how engineers work. They do not trouble themselves with the fundamental concepts of physics, but very successfully use calculation formulas which are derived from them. They are not at all bothered about the fact that many formulas have a single general nature, but this does not stop them from competently applying each of them to a specific task. The same can be said of physicians and basic biology."

"God, I have just one more question."

"Go on."

"If all processes in living matter simply boil down to the Law of Gene Preservation, why do not human communities get rid of their older members, who are no longer capable of procreation. Why don't we drive them out like they do in the animal world?"

"Why assume that things have always been as they are now? In ancient times when the human lifestyle differed little from that of animals, there were various ways of getting rid of infirm parents, such as taking them out to die in the so-called 'valleys of death.' All peoples have practised this at some point in their history and in some cultures, a record of it still survives in myths and legends."

"Then, God, what brought this terrible barbaric tradition to an end?"

"It lasted for quite long a long time and ended only after I singled man out from the rest of the natural world, giving to him a new quality from which morality subsequently evolved. This put an end to traditions such as these and gave rise to many others."

"What was the new quality?"

"I'll tell you more about this a little later when you begin to study the human beings specifically."

"Ok. Do you know, God, during these past four days, I have learned so much that I feel I should take a breather and reflect on it all. I need time to ponder and decide which phenomena in nature may or may not be explained based only on the Law of Gene Preservation. I think it would be a good idea if we took a break for a week."

"See you next week then. Have a rest, questioning one."

CONVERSATION 5. GENE PRESERVATION AND ABRAHAM

"So, how did your week go?"

"God, hello! You'll see in a moment how my week has gone. I was able to explain a huge amount using the Law of Gene Preservation and I want to place before your judgement everything I have concluded so far. I'll begin, as always, with a question. It is a question that has concerned me since childhood and it concerns the test to which You subjected Abraham when You commanded him to sacrifice his son Isaac in order to test the strength of his love and faith. Besides the fact that the story itself is so painful, it is totally alogical!

If the one thing that You have bestowed upon all living matter is the Law of Gene Preservation, then I would expect love and faithfulness to You to be best expressed in the fulfilment of the Law of Gene Preservation!"

"You understand correctly."

"Well then, to murder one's own son is surely not proof of a man's love for God but quite the opposite, it is to kill that love! Is it not written: '*and God blessed them, and God said to them: be fruitful and multiply, and replenish the Earth.*'? How could you order such an act? How could you even conceive of such a thing?"

"You think it was my idea?"

"Well, whose idea was it then? It is written in all three Abrahamic religions that You commanded Abraham to sacrifice Isaac and people have been reading and believing that for more than a thousand years!"

"Ask yourself, who could have made up the rest. Think about it!"

"No, surely it could not have been…"

"Exactly!"

"You know, God, let's finish here today. I don't think I can continue after that. I need to get over it…"

"See you tomorrow then."

CONVERSATION 6. GENE PRESERVATION AND THE JEWISH PHENOMENON

"God, I think I have found a clue to answering a question that is often discussed in society today: Why are the Jews so successful? Have You really endowed the Jews with special abilities?"

"Well, what do you think?"

"First, God, I'd like to tell you what the Jews themselves think. They believe that the persecution for millennia of the Jews by the Gentiles has developed in them a special intelligence, a special way of thinking and ability to survive under any conditions."

"Do you agree?"

"No! Gipsies all around the world have been persecuted no less than the Jews any they did not become 'the Jews.' The answer, in my view, is not that the persecution of the Jews has made them any more successful, but that the Jews have drawn the right conclusions from their experience of persecution: *to successfully fulfil the Law of Gene Preservation, that is, to firmly protect and pass on one's genes, one must invest everything in one's children, their health, upbringing and education,* so that the children receive specialised knowledge and skills of a higher level than those around them. I would only add that I have never witnessed any other nation who lived for the sake of their children as fanatically as the Jews do, or in other words, who have so fanatically fulfilled the Law of Gene Preservation. I would also add, that in a traditional Jewish family the education of children, in the sense of preparing them for their future life, is mainly overseen by the father, and this again distinguishes the Jews from other nations."

"There is still another component to 'Jewish success', but you will learn about that later."

"Ok. Bye for now then?"

"Yes, bye for now!"

CONVERSATION 7. GENE PRESERVATION AND MONOGAMOUS MARRIAGE

"God, today I heard something about the appearance of the family that even you probably don't know."

"What?"

"Sorry, God, I forgot myself. Indeed, until yesterday it was thought that monogamous marriage was a historical development of polygamous marriage in connection with the emergence of private property and the need to pass on property by inheritance. Just a few days ago a group of paleoanthropologists from University College London, who are conducting research into the family structure of primates, proved conclusively that the reason the ancients shifted to monogamous marriage was so that married couples, in which the husband was certain of his paternity, could protect their children from other aggressive males, who like lions in a pride would be capable of killing their competitor's offspring[3].

And so, monogamous marriage was created with the sole purpose of fulfilling the Law of Gene Preservation.

Again and again, we come back to the Law of Gene Preservation!

Today, there is a much less physical threat to children from men who are not their biological fathers and so the institution of marriage has weakened. The Law of Gene Preservation requires that parents not only protect their children's lives but also bring them up until they reach reproductive age and are capable of social

---

3 Opie, Dr Kit. Evolution of monogamy in humans the result of infanticide risk — See more at: https://www.ucl.ac.uk/news/news-articles/0713/30072013-evolution-of-monogamy#sthash.eFsbk8Xn.dpuf. *University College London.* [Internet] 30 July 2013. https://www.ucl.ac.uk/news/news-articles/0713/30072013-evolution-of-monogamy.

adaptation. Monogamous marriage is the best possible means of achieving this. *I would even refer to marriage as a joint venture for gene preservation because this is the main goal of any marriage.*

I have another question, Lord. If the Law of Gene Preservation is naturally fulfilled by man according to a programme which You have granted, why is it that throughout the world the wedding ritual is celebrated in such a festive manner. Is it a rite for the beginning of the fulfilment of the programme? Is a wedding not a private matter between the two people getting married, and perhaps their parents' families at most?

The Law of Gene Preservation was given to the individual, not to society as a whole. So why must it necessarily be a source of happiness for a larger number of relatives and close friends? Why does society always welcome a marriage and treat it such great respect?"

"This is our seventh conversation about the Law of Gene Preservation. Would not you like to try and answer this question yourself?"

"Ok, I'll try. I think it can be explained quite simply actually.

Throughout its history the collective survival of the human group has depended on the human resource, that is, the number of its members. This resource was essential during times of war with other tribes that arose over territorial disputes, acquiring new territories and retaining existing ones. Over time and right up until the 20th century, man's methods of livelihood have been extensive requiring ever new lands and resources. That is why when one tribe fought with another, similar in race, language and religion, the victors often sought to assimilate members of the new tribe rather than to destroy them.

And still, nothing so reliably increases the tribe's resource, as the maximum possible fulfilment by its members of childbearing age of the Law of Gene Preservation. That is why mankind has invented the wedding ritual and so happily prepares for it. That is why people have always treated mothers of many children with respect, and the state has created various benefits to help mothers look after their children.

Even today, when human economic management is shifting from extensive to intensive forms, and in some regions of the Earth has led to severe overpopulation, the fact of belonging to a large, powerful nation gives the individual confidence in the certainty of their existence, as well as significant privileges. But most importantly, people have always understood that it is only as a member of the largest and strongest tribe-nation, that they realistically increase their chances of protecting their own genes.

Are you satisfied with my answer, Lord?"

"In principle, yes."

"Then, until tomorrow."

CONVERSATION 8. GENE PRESERVATION AND HOMOSEXUALITY

"Hello, God! There is another 'fashionable' topic, which we cannot avoid talking about - Homosexuality in nature."

"No topic is taboo between us."

"Until recently, scientists believed that homosexuality was a result of gene mutation, but they could not identify any gene that in its 'healthy' condition would pass on heterosexuality, and in its 'mutated' condition, homosexuality. Recently though, scientists from the University of Tennessee, California and Uppsala University, Sweden, have shown that the development of homosexuality is affected not the genetic code itself, but by an error in the reading of it[4]. A mathematical model was constructed, which showed that the probability of this error is constant and corresponds to the percentage of homosexuals and lesbians in human society."

"Are you going to read me a lecture on popular genetics?"

"God forbid! I'm a complete amateur when it comes to biology. I just wanted to share what I drew from that information."

"And what did you draw from it? I'm listening."

"The first important thing, God, is that ***homosexuality, albeit probabilistic, is still hereditary. And the second thing is that the probability of inheritance is constant and small.***"

"Congratulations, you have worked out another question."

---

4 *Homosexuality as a Consequence of Epigenetically Canalized Sexual Development.* William R. Rice, Urban Friberg and Sergey Gavrilets. The Quarterly Review of Biology. Chicago: The University of Chicago Press, 2012. Vol. 87. No. 4 (December 2012). P. 343–368.

"But that is not why I began this conversation. To hell with (oops, sorry God!) the cause and mechanism for homosexuality. I have never been able to understand why the majority of people, for the most part throughout human history have been so hostile in their attitude to homosexuals, persecuting them and even physically destroying them, as was the case for example in Nazi Germany. And now the world has suddenly become very tolerant of homosexuality, and, what is more, Western countries are racing each other to allow same-sex marriages."

"And do you understand why that is now?"

"Yes, God, I do! Again, as always, it comes down to the Law of Gene Preservation! Whether they were conscious of it or not, in following the Law of Gene Preservation as the main principle of their existence, people intuitively felt that homosexual (and lesbian) love posed a mortal threat because of the lack of fertility of a same-sex relationship! People were haunted by the fear that homosexuality might spread like an epidemic and lead to the complete extinction of mankind. This is the reason for millennia of the severe persecution of homosexuals."

"Right. So how do you explain the fact that the relationship to homosexuality is changing in the West at its very core?"

"It is because a broad scientific awareness, above all in Western countries, has led to the realisation firstly, that *homosexuality is neither a conscious evil vice, nor is it contagious; and secondly, that the small number and stable percentage of homosexuals in the population poses no threat to the Law of Gene Preservation,* at least within the context of human society. How am I doing?"

"Not bad! So do you welcome the processes taking place in western countries or do you disapprove?"

"I neither welcome them nor judge them. That is not my task. I am simply stating what I observe around me and am trying to understand it."

"Then let that be all for today?"

"Yes, see you tomorrow!"

CONVERSATION 9. GENE PRESERVATION AND REPRODUCTIVE BEAUTY. GENDER PREFERENCES AND BEHAVIOUR IN ANIMALS AND HUMANS

"Hello! Have you been delving into things a lot this week?"

"Yes, quite a lot it would seem and I have a lot of new questions. I promised, God, to give You examples from my own real and virtual life, of things which I could not understand previously, but can now easily explain with the help of the Law of Gene Preservation. Let's take mating whales as our first example.

Usually, ichthyologists will tell you that a female whale will lie on the surface of the water, and begin actively flapping her fins until all male whales within the vicinity of the sound have gathered around her. When they approach, the female swims away, pursued by the males who compete with each other as they swim, often fighting violently, sometimes to the death. When only one male remains, the female swims away with him deep into the ocean to mate.

When I first heard about the 'heat run' I was immediately struck as to why the female would instigate such a bloody, nuptial contest, in which the remaining whales either die or are severely maimed? After all, could she not have swum away with the first whale to appear in response to the call of the basic instinct? No! In the case of the heat, the basic instinct is irrelevant! The female is selecting the strongest gene, that she may more reliably preserve her own. She is following the God-given Law of Gene Preservation! Marriage tournaments take place in virtually the same manner among all animals.

Primatologists have described an example of something similar. The ageing leader of a troop of monkeys jealously guarded his harem. A young adult leader began to make claims on one of the young females. The old alpha male made as if to give the younger male a fight but soberly assessing his chances, humbly accepted the situation. And the young leader left the troop with his prize. Several more young females joined the pair believing that their chances of passing on their own genes would be greater with the younger male. Here we see the undoubtable precedence of the Law of Gene Preservation over the instinct to preserve the species or herd.

It is exactly the same with people, so why have we traditionally condemned women who behave in this way?"

"Well, how exactly do things work with people?"

"It is exactly the same, God! Perhaps it does not happen as openly or as honestly as it does among animals, but essentially the same thing happens. Due to erroneously constructed moral principles, people are often ashamed of their natural preferences and forced to sanctimoniously justify their choice in fear of public condemnation and ridicule. People tend to choose their sexual partner in the same way as individuals in the animal kingdom, with the one primary objective of finding the best and most reliable way of preserving their own genes. If in primitive times a woman sought to find a strong warrior or tribal leader who would protect their common genes in the future better than anyone else, then today she will choose a rich and prominent man with exactly the same goal in mind. Moreover, a woman learns very quickly to see a handsome prince in a rich and prominent man! Many women have admitted to me that they are attracted to a man with a strong intellect and I find it very hard to imagine that this may somehow be connected to physiology. I think that women are subconsciously triggered by the expectation that a man with a strong intellect will achieve social success.

It is precisely because of the Law of Gene Preservation, albeit unconsciously, that men have since primordial times striven for power, wealth and public success, and as we would say today, a successful career.

Even in the animal world, alpha males have a preferential right to reproduction and to the protection of their offspring, and in some wolf packs or lion prides that right even becomes exclusive.

Why have men always been attracted to wide-hipped, full-breasted women, the kind the old masters so loved to paint? Is it, as medical scientists would say today, that these external qualities almost unmistakably speak of a woman's reproductive health, or perhaps one could say her reproductive beauty, and men instinctively and accurately sense that?

American scientists once conducted the following experiment. A group of nine women participating in the experiment were given identical t-shirts to wear and were asked not to take them off for two days. Among the participants were women who, from a male point of view, would be considered very beautiful, not particularly beautiful and not at all beautiful. Then the t-shirts were placed in identical, numbered bags and given to nine male volunteers who had never met each other or the other nine women before. The men were led into a room, one by one, and asked to smell the bags. All the men accurately identified the most beautiful of the nine women by their smell!

This can only be explained by the fact that reproductive beauty is determined not only visually, but also odorously! In another experiment, instead of t-shirts, men were given recordings of women's voices to listen to, and the experiment yielded the same result, i.e. notions of beauty in visual, odorous and audio form all coincided, and all together can be referred to simply as a woman's reproductive beauty.

God, I also realise now why notions of female beauty differ so greatly among men and women. Women will truly admire the beauty in another woman, while a man may not see anything special in her at all. The reason for this is very simple. A woman perceives the beauty of another woman in the form of her nose, lips or eyes; in some standard of beauty imposed on her by the external world of paintings, photographs and films. By contrast, a man fails to see or understand any of that but by some animal-like instinct, picks up on her reproductive beauty, to which another woman would naturally be totally indifferent.

As you can see, again and again, things come back to the Law of Gene Preservation.

The other thing that I have come to understand, God, is why gender upbringing has differed since ancient times, and in particular, why women have been brought up to observe absolute fidelity to their husbands while this condition has not been demanded of men."

"And why has the style of upbringing differed according to gender?"

"Because by virtue of the different public and domestic status enjoyed by men and women, the same Law of Gene Preservation required totally different sexual behaviour in each sex. Spending most of their time outside the home, hunting, and obeying the Law of Gene Preservation, a man had to scatter his seed as wide and as often as possible, because, in the past, infant survival rates were extremely low. Spending all her time at home (in the cave), a woman was supposed to avoid the intrusion of another man's gene into the family, a requirement that was jealously watched over by her husband's relatives, with whom, as a rule, she lived. Once she had conceived her husband's child, she was expected to make every effort to protect it, cutting off any other contacts. All this required women to be totally focused on her husband and the family.

Today in the countries of Europe and North America, where men and women are genuinely equal in terms of public and domestic rights and where they share almost the same lifestyle, differences in gender behaviour are gradually disappearing. Now it is clear that the distinction between men and women represents a consequence of differences in social status, rather than their physical nature, and so the distinction between them will disappear as differences in status also fade. One can observe the same dynamics occurring in some Asian countries, which are following the European path of development."

"Is that everything?"

"No, not quite. Almost everything I observe around me can be explained by the Law of Gene Preservation though there are so many examples I don't have the energy to go into them all today."

"Then, until tomorrow."

"Yes, see you tomorrow!"

CONVERSATION 10. GENE PRESERVATION, LEVIRATE, SORORATE AND THE TABOO ON COUSIN MARRIAGE

"God, let's talk today about traditions and taboos related to the Law of Gene Preservation."

"Yes, why not? That's an interesting topic!"

"In ancient times, in conditions of cold and hunger and the complete absence of any medical treatment, gene preservation was an exceedingly difficult task. And even high birth rates could not guarantee the fulfilment of the Law of Gene Preservation due to equally high rates of infant mortality. People were plagued by the constant fear of being left without offspring, without an heir.

When there was no possible way of preserving their own gene, they tried to preserve the genes of the closest blood relative. For example, if a married man died leaving no children, the task of 'preserving the genes of the deceased' fell on the shoulders of a brother or other close relative. It is in these conditions that the custom of levirate arose among many nations. The ancient Jews called it Yavam, the ancient Kazakhs, Amenger. According to the levirate custom, it was the duty of the brother-in-law, the brother of the deceased husband, to marry the childless widow. This past custom becomes particularly interesting in the light of modern scientific research which points to high probabilities of genetic overlap between brothers. The Kazakhs applied the Amenger marriage custom when a deceased brother already had children, with the same purpose of preserving the genes of the deceased.

It seems to me that attempts made by some researchers to explain the levirate custom as polyandry, the law of inheritance or as some other legal concern are quite misguided.

If the wife of a childless couple died, for example in childbirth, some cultures practised the custom of sororate marriage (the mirror image of levirate), in which her widower-husband would marry his wife's sister. People also turned to the sororate custom in cases of a wife's sterility, moreover, the first marriage was preserved.

In ancient times, the Kazakhs had another custom by which a family would give one of their children when they were still very young to a married brother or sister who as a couple could not conceive.

God, the Law of Gene Preservation not only gives rise to customs encouraging the actions of people who develop it but also generates taboos on other actions that might contradict the Law.

In early times, people noticed that marriage between close relatives could lead to the serious risk of transmitting a variety of hereditary abnormalities, e.g., the birth of a handicapped child or even an immature delivery. As a result of such observations, the legal system of almost all countries in the world forbids incest as marital relations between blood relatives. In most countries, legislation also forbids marriage between cousins.

As skilful breeders, Kazakh nomadic herders have always been well aware of the implications of closely related breeding and have forbidden marriage between relatives with common ancestors within seven generations. As a result, cases of autism, Down's syndrome, breast cancer and many other hereditary diseases are much less frequently observed among the Kazakh people.

Today has turned out to be more of a monologue than a dialogue, God, hasn't it?"

"Yes, but that's alright."

CONVERSATION 11. GENE PRESERVATION. GOOD AND EVIL, ADULTERY AND JEALOUSY

"Hello! What would you like to talk to me about today?"

"Today, God, I would like us to talk about good and evil, once again in the context of the Law of Gene Preservation. It is an inexhaustible and subjective theme which man has spent the best part of history trying to define. The concepts of good and evil held by different social groups have often clashed leading to violent controversy. Attempts to resolve the differences have often served as a catalyst for major change and social development.

It seems to me that the basic concept of good and evil in human society is another aspect of the Law of Gene Preservation.

For centuries society has held the woman's role as mother in high esteem. In her honour songs and poems are composed. Nowhere is society's respect for motherhood so eloquently expressed as in images by artists and sculptors of the Madonna and child. Governments pass laws to protect the importance of motherhood. When parents fail to protect and care for their offspring, the state may deprive them of their parental rights. The Law of Gene Preservation is the priority of the race and thus is always reflected in society's laws and customs. Nobody would ever object to the slogan 'It's in the best interests of the children.' In times of war or natural disaster, the children are always evacuated first.

A huge percentage of world literature is consciously or unconsciously devoted to the theme of the Law of Gene Preservation, for example, Chinghiz Aitmatov's novel 'Spotted Dog, Running Along The Seashore.' A teenage boy, his father, his childless, bachelor uncle and his grandfather go to sea in a boat to hunt for seal but are caught in a storm. They lose control of the boat which is carried out to open sea by the wind and current and there they drift for days on end. One night when food and water supplies are at the point of running out the grandfather quietly disappears from the boat, followed by the childless uncle and finally, the boy's father. The boat carrying the boy, who survives thanks to what little food and water supplies remained, is finally washed up on a native shore. Is not this story a hymn to the Law of Gene Preservation?

If service to the Law of Gene Preservation is acknowledged by man as an expression of the highest good, then a crime against it must be considered the worst of evils.

I know of one example that occurred in Russia. A few years ago, huge crowds of residents from the city of Bryansk set out to storm the local police station armed with sticks and stones. They were willing to risk their freedom for the chance to take the law into their own hands and subject a young family being held in the station to mob-justice. Why? The young couple had not robbed anyone, threatened any of the townspeople, the adults, their children or their relatives. So what caused the local people to react so passionately? What happened?

The young couple had committed the worst crime known to nature. They had murdered their one-year-old daughter.

We are taught, that to kill is a crime and great sin, but we can be quite indifferent to the daily news in which we learn of the killing of thousands. Yes, we are willing to fight to the death for the lives of our loved ones, and above all, our children but in this case, the matter concerned someone else's child. Moreover, we are taught in life not to get involved in the upbringing of other people's children, even if it seems to be excessively severe. The young couple who murdered their child were not maniac rapists who would pose a threat to the other children in the community. At that time, this kind of murder was practically unheard of and so people had no conditioned response to the crime.

What so enraged the hundreds of people who simultaneously rose up to destroy evil in the form of the young parents? The monsters who killed their own child encroached on the most sacred of sacred in the natural world. They had encroached on the most important Covenant of God, bestowed upon all living things; they went against the Law of Gene Preservation.

And the residents of Bryansk sensed it with animal-like instinct. For the same reason, to the present day, in some countries, abortion is still considered a grave sin. Now I'd like to move on to the nature of jealousy.

The Law of Gene Preservation also lies at the root of jealousy.

A man feels jealous of his wife, because he fears that she might, unbeknown to him, bring the genes of another man into the family, and he would have to feed and educate another man's child. A woman feels jealous of her husband because she fears that if he has children with other women on the side, part of his love, efforts and income will go to them, depriving their common genes of their legitimate share.

That is why adultery had always been perceived so negatively in traditional societies. The punishment for adultery was often death, for example by stoning. This form of punishment still exists in the world today in countries with a totalitarian morality.

Exactly the same kind of jealousy can be seen in the animal world.

How are you finding my lecture so far?"

"Not bad at all. Your understanding of things is good."

"There are some things I don't understand though, for instance, I don't understand why attitudes to extra-marital affairs are changing so radically, particularly in countries with a spirit of liberal morality, the path of which, all other countries appear to be following. Why don't we ever hear about Othello and Desdemona anymore? Why is the attitude to jealousy in these increasingly veering towards the opinion that jealousy is a sin? Jealousy, after all, stems from the Law of Gene Preservation, which You have given. Generally speaking, whereas the Law of Gene Preservation is enough to facilitate a principled explanation of the behaviour of animals, it is clearly lacking as an explanation for human behaviour. This requires something else, although quite what exactly, I am not certain."

"We will talk about that later when we come to study the human being in more depth. You are not ready for that yet."

"Sooner rather than later!"

"Bye for now!"

CONVERSATION 12. GENE PRESERVATION OR PROTECTION OF THE OFFSPRING? GRANDPARENTS AND GRANDCHILDREN

"Greetings, God, at this pre-dawn hour! Will today's conversation be our last on the Law of Gene Preservation?"

"Yes, we have talked about this topic enough. I have a final question for you though, to check how accurately you have understood. In all the examples you have cited, living creatures fight fiercely to protect their offspring. Would it not have been more relevant for us to converse on the Law of the Protection of Offspring, rather than the Law of Gene Preservation?"

"I don't think so. These ideas are very similar but they are not identical and I can give you several examples to illustrate the difference. Scientists have witnessed how a mother whale responds when a killer whale attacks a humpback calf. The mother-whale will fight desperately to protect her calf. If the calf is fatally wounded and beyond saving, the mother whale will swim away to save herself, that she may conceive more young in the future and pass on her genes to her offspring. There are similar examples of this type of behaviour among people. When a young mother loses her only child and is inconsolable with grief, her relatives will advise her to conceive another child as soon as possible, knowing that only the birth of another child, or in other words, only gene preservation will heal her despair.

In another example, a panda gave birth to two cubs in a zoo in China. The mother-panda did not have enough milk to feed both her cubs. She refused to feed the weaker of the two so that her milk went to the stronger cub. A female eagle will do the same. Unable to feed two fledgeling chicks, she will give all her feed to the stronger fledgeling.

Another example concerns a tragic, crazy, do-or-die moment in a person's life which is essentially very similar.

I remember an eerie story of a man who lived his childhood through the great Kazakh famine of the 1930s. Communists from Moscow forcibly deprived the local population of their cattle, sentencing millions to death by starvation. The mother of the narrator, who had two small children, a boy and a girl, was maddened by hunger like everyone else. She left the village and walked in the direction of the town in search of food. On the way, which led through the open steppe, the poor family was attacked by a pack of hungry wolves. Foreseeing the imminent death of the three of them, the mother made a horrific decision. She left the younger, weaker child, her daughter, to the wolves and as a result managed to escape with her son. This tragic story is another clear example of the Law of Gene Preservation in practice. I was just going to say, 'please God, don't let anyone have to face a choice like that again', and then I remembered, You gave the laws of life but You do not interfere in the details of life's unfolding."

"You are quite right when you say that this was 'a crazy, do-or-die moment.' Surely you must see that people differ slightly from animals in their fulfilment of the Law of Gene Preservation. You must also have noticed how attentively a mother will care for the weakest of her children giving them the larger portion of food, and greater nursing and attention? You must see how parents worry most about the future of their least talented children?"

"Yes, I know, but why is that?"

"It is because with the birth and development of the human soul, people began to have an awareness of their own humanity, of which we shall speak more later."

"God, why is it you think that people were not always aware of their own humanity?"

"Well, you remember the ancient Spartans, who, blindly obeying the instinct of gene preservation, threw their invalid children over the edge of steep cliffs? The main reason the Spartans did this was not because they thought integrating disabled children into society would be problematic. They did it because they did not want to risk spreading what they erroneously feared might have been a hereditary disability. There are numerous examples of similar situations in ancient history and for that matter in more recent times. Have I made my point?"

"Yes, God."

"Then I have just one more question for you. Can you explain why birth rates are so low in the countries of Europe and North America on the one hand, and so high in the countries of Asia and Africa on the other? Tell me, is the human relationship to the Law of Gene Preservation changing over time, or not?"

"In essence, no, but in form, yes! Differences in birth rates have nothing to do with the continent, so much as the level of development of a given nation. In economics, agriculture and technology, as in the matter of gene preservation, 'extensive' practices are gradually replacing 'intensive' practices.

In centuries past, high infant mortality rates meant that giving birth to as many children as possible served as the most reliable guarantee for successfully passing on one's genes. Today, in developed countries, a parent's priority is not the number of children they bring into the world, so much as the quality of preparation for life they can give to their offspring; ensuring that they are in the best of health and receive the highest standard of education possible in order to maximise their future chances of survival in society.

Birth rates are also falling in the developed countries of Asia which only goes to show that the reason for falling birth rates has less to do with the continent than with a country's position on the arrow of time. Is that right?"

"Yes. So shall we end there then?"

"No, hang on a moment. God, can you explain why human parents, who have fulfilled the Law of Gene Preservation do not stop there? Why does the single status of boomerang kids worry them so much? Why do they long for grandchildren, and once they have them, succeed in loving them no less, if not more, than their own children?"

"I'm afraid you have not fully understood the Law of Gene Preservation after all. It is about the preservation of the genes, not the preservation of the offspring. Do you see the difference? When adult sons and daughters fail to marry, the human parent, unlike all other living creatures, is very well aware that their genetic line may die out. The inverse is also true. The more grandchildren a parent has, the more confidently they feel that their genes are protected. When grandchildren appear in the family, the Grandparents' love, care and attention pass from their own children onto the grandchildren. This fact is often explained by the simple fact that the grandchildren are young and weak still, and therefore in need of more care and protection than the grandparents' adult children. This is true of course, but the real motivating factor lies in the fact that it is now the grandchildren, who will continue to pass on the grandparents' genes in the future. Do you understand?"

"Yes. Your explanation is quite straightforward. I am thinking ahead a bit actually. Now I understand why people are so concerned that their descendants should preserve the family name. They see the family name as a type of Gene Preservation, albeit illusory! Your explanation also sheds light on the traditional preference among patriarchal peoples for a boy child rather than a daughter as the boy would continue to carry the family name. Traditional social distinctions between the future role of boys and girls coupled with an ignorance of genetics has prevented people from even guessing at their equality in the matter of preserving the parent gene. Have I understood the Law of Gene Preservation correctly now?"

"Yes. So sum up the topic if you can."

"Ok. *The sole purpose of the existence of all life on Earth, excluding man, is self-reproduction.* Procreation is a fundamental purpose for human beings, but it is not their sole purpose."

"Ok. Now I see that you are ready to discuss the second law, which I have given to mankind so we will conclude our discussion of the Law of Gene Preservation."

"God, wait! What I don't understand is why we spent so much time discussing the Law of Gene Preservation in the animal world and its parallel manifestation in the human world. Could we not have focused on the human race right from the start?"

"It seems, human being, that you have not understood our conversations after all! The most important idea that has emerged from the numerous examples we have looked at, is that in the context of the Law of Gene Preservation, human beings represent an inseparable part of the entire animal world and are in no way distinguishable from it. So rather than speaking in terms of the parallels that exist between animals and humans, it would be more appropriate to talk about the organic membership of the human race to the entire biological world, although I repeat, this principle only applies to the Law of Gene Preservation. Are we clear now?"

"I am getting there gradually..."

"In that case, until we meet again!"

"He who increases knowledge increases sorrow..."

Ecclesiastes

"But gains Freedom..."

Anonymous

"Free at last! Free at last!
Praise be to Almighty God - We are free!"

From an African-American spiritual

PART II
THE LAW OF FREEDOM OF CHOICE

CONVERSATION 13. THE LAW OF FREEDOM OF CHOICE. HOMO ELIGENTI

"Hello, God! Finally, the day that I have been waiting for has arrived and I can ask you the question I have been dying to ask: What did You bestow upon man to distinguish him from the rest of the living world? Is it the soul?"

"No, that's not quite it. I know that people love this word and that your priests, writers, poets, and most of all moralists, especially like to talk about the soul. But I do not want to begin today's conversation with something vague that lacks clear definition or a simple means of verification. It is no secret that people understand the soul and spirituality in different ways, and so their arguments on this topic have never abated. God, well, me, being willing, we shall return to the topic of the soul and show how it evolved 'out of nothing' but later, when you are better prepared."

"I agree that the soul is a complex topic, God, no less because scientists are now discovering empathy in some animal species. Does this animal empathy not point to the beginnings of soul? Perhaps the difference between animals and man is that man possesses the power of speech? But again, many animals have been shown to have the beginnings of a second signal system. I struggle to find an answer to this question."

"Ask yourself, what do you have that permanently distinguishes your behaviour in all ways from the behaviour of animals? What have you been doing or trying to do from a very young age, from the moment that you began to be aware of self, when you sit at the table and demand one type of food and refuse to eat another; when you prefer to wear one item of clothing rather than another; when you go outside and play with one group of friends rather than another and when you choose a husband or wife; when you reach adulthood and go to the polls to vote for head of state or a local government candidate, if of course, you live in a free country.

What do you have to do every day, every hour and even every minute, for instance, when you start your day and choose whether to get up or doze for a while, when you go to work via the same road every morning or choose one of many possible routes, when you chat with friends or colleagues about topics you find interesting, when you listen to your favourite music, and so on, right up until the end of the day, when you choose whether to watch one more interesting program on TV or go up to bed?

Are you not constantly in a state of choice, large or small? Even now, you are choosing to talk to me, whereas you could turn and walk away."

"God! Why didn't I guess straight away! You gave man freedom of choice! It's true, as human beings we are constantly in a state of choice, which I can tell You, is not very easy and at times is downright tricky. Yes, this makes us fundamentally different from animals. Let's call it the Law of Freedom of Choice."

"Ok!"

"Tell me, God, is that all You gave us? Nothing else?"

"That's all."

"What about the intellect, soul, morality even? What about craft, science, art?"

"All these things people have developed of their own accord, thanks to freedom of choice. To be honest, I am not entirely certain of what words like soul and morality mean."

"Are you serious? I could not have imagined that You ..."

"Consider these things yourself. Tell me about them at our future meetings and I will listen."

"Then my next question, God, is this: Why did you give us freedom of choice?"

"I was bored all alone in the Universe. Now I find life much more interesting, observing you all, and perhaps I understand myself better too..."

"Are you saying that in giving us freedom of choice you have in fact made us equal to God?"

"No, not quite. I have given you the opportunity to become as close to me as you desire to do so. And this again will depend on the choice of each."

"Do You know, Lord, that the closer a person tries to get to You, the more they use freedom of choice for the purpose of developing their spiritual and intellectual world, the less they actually believe in You? Is this not a paradox?"

"It's not a paradox! I don't believe in anyone either!"

"Really! Then let me ask you something else, God. Do You possess freedom of choice to the absolute degree?"

"Not anymore. *Having created the world as it is, I can no longer change the physical laws on which it rests.* But let's talk about that in a separate conversation about the Universe."

"Ok, good. So, tell me, God, if I have understood You correctly, having received the freedom of choice from You, from God, we, human beings are responsible for all our actions throughout our entire life?"

"Exactly! Now you are all totally responsible for everything in your life!"

"And you don't have any influence on people's lives anymore?"

"I don't influence anything - nothing at all! What would be the point of giving you freedom of choice if I then tried to exert my own influence on your life? It comes down to one thing: either you are free in every choice you make, or, like all other animals, you are evolving in accordance with Darwin's Theory of Evolution, yielding only to the Law of Gene Preservation. A third is not given as they say!"

"What about the saying *'not one hair of his head shall fall to the ground unless it be God's will'*?"

"Complete nonsense! As if I had nothing better to do than look after your hair!"

"You have quite a sense of humour, God."

"You bet! It's what keeps me going!"

"But, God, if you do not intervene in anything that happens in a person's life, then logically it is tantamount to saying, that for people, you do not exist?"

"That's how it is. And it does not worry me in the least."

"So does that mean that it is pointless asking You for anything?"

"Totally!"

"There are so many people on the Earth who pray to You, who look to You for comfort and support, and sing songs of praise to

You. Doctors even confirm that prayer has a beneficial impact on human health. So what happens now? Are they all to be left without any support?"

"If people like to pray, if as you say, they find comfort in prayer, let them pray. They are free to choose. But I repeat what I said. People need to know the truth. And as far as the singing of praises goes, ask yourself, what is that to me?"

"My last question then, God is this: Why is it, that having received the gift of freedom of choice I cannot always apply it? Why is it that having chosen a solution to a problem, I often encounter difficulties? It conflicts for instance with the freedom of choice in others and becomes impossible to carry out?"

"Would you have preferred it if I had only given freedom of choice to you personally? I too had to choose whether to give freedom of choice to a selected few or to give it to all indiscriminately. I consciously chose the latter and I had weighty reasons for doing so. I wish to stress once again that *freedom of choice is not given to peoples or nations as a whole, but to every person individually.* This does not mean that for certain periods of time, freedom of choice cannot unite a people enabling them to achieve common goals or likewise, disunite a people. You're faced with this effect continually over the course of your own life."

"Tell me, Lord, how long ago did you endow people with freedom of choice?"

"It depends on how you look at it. On the one hand, your humanoid ancestors appeared on Earth quite a long time ago, millions of years ago in fact and lived, like all living matter, with the exclusive concern of protecting and passing on their genes. It is only a few tens of thousands of years ago that man received the freedom of choice."

"God, scientists have data that corroborate your words but instead of freedom of choice, they use the enigmatic term 'mind', for which it is difficult to give a clear, straightforward definition. It is difficult to find two people, whose view of the mental clarity of a third person fully coincide.

It seems to me, that instead of Homo Sapiens — 'Wise Man', it would be simpler to speak of Homo Eligenti — 'Choosing Man'.

Tell me, God, given that the gift of freedom of choice was bestowed upon all, why is it that people use it so differently?"

"Yes, the degree to which people understand and accept the Law of Freedom of Choice varies hugely, and in this, it is fundamentally different to the Law of Gene Preservation. Everyone who receives the freedom of choice chooses how to use it.

If you were to place all people human beings on one arrow of time according to the extent to which they use freedom of choice, then closer to the point striving into the future, would be those few, who live guided entirely by personal freedom of choice, who would be willing to give up their life even for the sake of freedom of choice.

Closer to the source, the starting point, would stand those of another kind, the many who feel no need for freedom of choice, for whom gene preservation is sufficient. Instead of relying on freedom of choice, such people obey the laws set out for them by others, laws not only granted in a legal sense but often instilled in the form of tradition, the observance of which can even be embellished to the point of ritual."

"So, it turns out then, God, that some people deprive others of Your divine gift of the freedom of choice? Why do the latter allow the former to deprive them of freedom of choice?"

"That's how it is. Don't forget though, that giving away one's freedom of choice to others is also a choice, and sadly, the choice is often voluntary! This is the choice of the slave! Do not judge these people too harshly, for historically speaking *homo eligenti* appeared relatively recently from beings who did not have freedom of choice.

The thing is that freedom of choice immediately gives rise to the problem of choice!

Nothing quite develops man as powerfully as the problem of choice. I remember how funny it was to look at people when I first bestowed freedom of choice upon them. When freedom of choice suddenly replaced life which had been univariate with life that was multivariate people were perplexed, frightened even, stumbling from side to side like blind kittens.

So many conflicts arose due to freedom of choice! It was as if the constant necessity to make a choice at every moment of daily life, in other words, the problem of choice increasingly burdened the brain. Gradually, at first slowly, slowly and then faster and faster the intellect began to develop eventually giving birth to all kinds of science.

Conflicts which arose between people on the grounds of the problem of choice in relationships gave birth to ethics and morality, in other words, they led to voluntary self-restraint of individual freedom of choice. It was this tendency which subsequently led to the birth of the soul.

But we are getting ahead of ourselves again.

The history of the evolution of the human race is essentially the history of the development of freedom of choice and the untiring effort human beings exert in order to expand personal freedom of choice. The hunger to reach adulthood which childhood experiences is a hunger to expand personal freedom of choice! And the fear of ageing people experience at middle age is a fear of inhibited freedom of choice!

Science, art, wanderlust, and all striving towards the unknown in general is simply the phenomenon of searching for the limits of individual freedom of choice. All civil liberties, such as freedom of thought, freedom of speech, freedom of religion, for which the best gave their lives, are nothing other than different manifestations of freedom of choice. Every one of them could serve as the topic of a separate conversation."

"God, I think I am beginning to understand what freedom of choice is, and now I have so many ideas leaping around my mind, sparking off other thoughts that it is difficult to focus. Here's one idea:

The level of a people's development is defined by the degree to which freedom of choice exists within it.

The more extensively the individual members of a society exercise their right to freedom of choice, the happier and more successful life in that society will generally be.

Compare how the peoples of Europe and North America live with the lifestyle of the majority of countries in Asia and Latin America. The difference tends to be erroneously attributed to the state of democracy in these countries as if democracy were a primary independent notion."

"What is democracy?"

"God, do you really not know what democracy is?"

"Well, of course, I hear what people talk about it. They call it 'people power' or something that like, but other than that, I am not entirely clear. I would not want you and me to start using 'clever' words and ideas that we have not agreed the meaning of. I would rather we stuck with the concepts of gene preservation and freedom of choice so that we can be completely clear in what we are trying to communicate."

"Ok then, God, I shall try to define it in context.

Democracy is when the basic needs of individual freedom of choice coincide among the majority of a given society, and the needs of the majority are met by the coming to power of their political representatives.

It's something like that. The key thing about democracy is not some abstract idea of 'people power', but rather the fact that the choices of the majority coincide. Would a person really be willing to die for some notion of 'people power' unless they expected it to validate their personal freedom of choice? I am beginning to get a sense of the direction in which humanity is evolving, and I think I can formulate it as a fundamental law, like the second law of thermodynamics."

"Stop, stop, stop! This time I am the one who is tired. We cannot cover everything in one conversation. Let's take things one step at a time. We've done enough for one day!"

"God, wait! I have just one small addition. You will like it I promise! I just wanted to say that people really do value and understand the meaning of the gift of freedom of choice which you have given them. For example, there was an American writer called John Steinbeck. In his novel, 'East of Eden', he discovered that in the biblical parable of Cain and Abel the words which You are supposed to have spoken to Cain after he had murdered his brother, are different in British and American translations of the Bible to the original Hebrew. What is a small difference in translation actually implies a huge difference in the meaning of Your words particularly with regard to freedom of choice.

In the English King James edition, Your words sound like a prediction: 'Thou shalt rule over him' (You will rule over sin) which would appear to mean that the men can go freely about their lives, knowing that the feeling of sin will be overcome automatically. In the American Standard translation, Your words sound like an order: 'Do Thou rule over him' (Rule over sin), which would appear to mean that men are obliged to obey God without a murmur of doubt. Only in the original Hebrew version, by saying: 'Thou mayest rule over him' (You may rule over sin), do You give man the freedom to make the difficult choice, whether to fight against sin or not! With just one Hebrew word 'timshel' ('Thou mayest') you communicate to man, that he always has freedom of choice.

Steinbeck writes:

> *'But 'Thou mayest'! Why, that makes a man great, that gives him stature with the gods, for in his weakness and his filth and his murder of his brother he has still the great choice.'*

> *'It is easy out of laziness, out of weakness, to throw oneself into the lap of deity, saying, 'I couldn't help it; the way was set.' But think*

of the glory of the choice! That makes a man a man. A cat has no choice, a bee must make honey. There's no godliness there...'[5]

I would like to add, God, just in case you were in any doubt, that people do genuinely value the gift of freedom of choice that you have given them and fight for it from the very first breath. The dissatisfied cry of a three year old at the kitchen table who refuses to eat porridge and demands sweets instead is exactly the same in nature as the protest of an adult male, climbing a barricade for the right to decide where, how and with whom he may live and what kind of business he may run.

There are no other reasons for human protest and there never have been.

All human protest is a protest against the infringement of Freedom of Choice.

Unfortunately, when people are born and brought up in a totalitarian regime, they gradually lose connection with their inherent and God-given capacity to protest against the suppression of freedom of choice, and often voluntarily and even gladly accept the path of a slave.

God, this is such a painful and tragic subject for me; let's talk about it in a separate conversation.

As you can see, God, we human beings try to make the right choices, but we do not always get it right, so do not be angry with us."

"I don't know anger. I am not angry, either at the animals for living in ignorance of freedom of choice, or at human beings for living according to their own choices."

---

5 Steinbeck, John Ernst East of Eden. Penguin Classics (2014) ISBN 978-0141394893

"Then this is my last question for today. Why did not you oversee the translation of the Bible?"

"You assume I oversaw the original?"

"Ah yes, I'm sorry, I forgot. Then, until next time?"

"Until next time!"

CONVERSATION 14. FREEDOM OF CHOICE, FREE LOVE AND TRUE LOVE

"God, now that I understand more about freedom of choice, the first thing that comes to mind is to ask You how the Law of Freedom of Choice overlays the Law of Gene Preservation. How are the two laws related?"

"Yes, this is perhaps the most interesting point. At first, I thought that man would simply have both, in contrast to other living matter. I admit, I thought that freedom of choice would simply complement the Law of Gene Preservation. I did not foresee that they would conflict."

"I have seen numerous examples, God, of people who, once married, deliberately limit their freedom of choice and personal self-development for the sake of the most important task that You have given us, to give birth to their offspring and prepare them for adulthood, that is, to fulfil the Law of Gene Preservation. In other words, the Law of Gene Preservation restrains freedom of choice and remains the priority for the human race, just as it represents the priority of all living matter. Is that right?"

"If only that were the case! You must also have seen examples where the inverse is true, where freedom of choice limits fulfilment of the Law of Gene Preservation? Perhaps less often, but nonetheless..."

"Are you talking about victims of alcoholism and drug abuse?"

"No, of course not! The people you mention are indeed victims, although it would be truer to say that they are rather victims of freedom of choice, of the inability to use it for their own benefit."

"I think I have worked out what kind of people You mean. You mean fanatics of the arts and sciences, revolutionaries, servants of various religious groups, people who are totally absorbed by a passion for the sake of which they consciously sacrifice all the normal joys of life, and above all, family, gene preservation."

"Exactly!"

"Yes, and yet only one fanatic in every thousand, if not in every million actually achieves the goal they set themselves fully realising their aspirations like, for example, the central character in 'The Moon and Sixpence' by William Somerset Maugham. The rest are doomed to a fate of broken lives filled with deprivation and failure. And nevertheless, individuals like these are born to every generation. Is freedom of choice really what lies at the root of their passion?"

"To a greater or lesser extent, everyone is susceptible to some passion or another, but only those who choose freely can consciously follow it."

"God! Why don't we begin today's conversation with the topic of so-called 'free love', sex that has no reproductive purpose? Let's look at the question of when, how and under which conditions the notion of 'free love' appeared. It is a phenomenon that fundamentally distinguishes man from the animal world for whom sex exists exclusively to fulfil Your will of gene preservation. And why did society condemn the phenomenon of 'free love' for millennia?"

"I must admit, that 'free love' was the first phenomenon I never really anticipated. Prior to Freedom of Choice, sex served the sole function of preserving human genes. It barely differed from sex among animals and was not coupled with emotional intimacy."

"I understand, God! From here I can pick up the thread myself. As individual freedom of choice developed, people became aware that although they did not always feel ready to continue their family line, they still experienced the passion, which You gave all life, for the purpose of gene preservation. There are many reasons to avoid the consequences of this kind of passion. The most important in today's world is that an individual is socially unprepared for the consequences, unprepared to provide and care for their own offspring, that is, to fully realise the Law of Gene Preservation.

There have been other reasons too, for instance, a person is unable to enter into marriage with the object of their passion and together fulfil the Law of Gene Preservation. Perhaps issues of convention, race or religion prevent it, or perhaps that person is already married. Then man discovered 'free love.' People learned various different methods of protecting themselves from the reproductive effects of sex. Notably, the first condom was invented more than a thousand years ago."

"Why was 'free love' frowned upon by society for so long?"

"For the same reason that homosexuality, prostitution and abortion which we have already discussed were not considered acceptable. People saw it as a threat to the Law of Gene Preservation! They thought that everyone would rush into having 'free love' and no one would fulfil the Law of Gene Preservation, which of course the practical reality of human life has proven false. Like all other living beings, man can never deny the Law You have given."

"That's pretty clear."

"In conclusion, I would like to add that the intimacy and secrecy of 'free love' and the turbulent emotions of those who engage in this kind of relationship have played a significant role in the development of the love genre in all fields of art.

It seems that with Your help, God, we have clarified this topic. The main result of our conversation today has been to clarify that even though 'free love' avoids fulfilment of the Law of Gene Preservation, it has not influenced the Law in any way. Like all living creatures, people strive to fulfil the law, to have children who will outlive them and to preserve their genes on Earth. It is just that, unlike other living beings, man has learned to respond to the Law of Gene Preservation in a conscious fashion."

"What other topic do you have planned for today?"

"Oh, this one's really interesting, God. It's called love."

"And what is love?"

"Don't You know what love is?"

"No..."

"Wow! Talking to You gets more and more interesting as we go along."

"Can you get to the point and define love?"

"God, I don't think I can give a very good definition of love. There will be as many definitions of love, as there are people who have experienced it. The nature of love is inexplicable. A whole mountain of literature has been written about love, but a definition of love does not become any clearer for it. No one knows how love appears, and where and why it later disappears even in cases of requited love. No one knows why love visits some on many occasions, and never visits others their entire life. The history of the arts is to a large degree indebted to this feeling. Recently, scientists have sought an explanation for love, reporting on biochemical processes, and the compatibility of certain physiological characteristics. But how can those things explain love at first sight?"

"You are rather dragging out your introduction."

"Ok, then God, following the principle we have agreed upon, according to which we will only use the simplest and most easily verifiable definitions, I shall try and give the kind of definition of love, which I think the majority of people would agree with.

In my opinion, love is a person's ardent passion to preserve their genes exclusively with one single representative of the opposite sex, humanity's entire other half.

This is the difference between love and the straightforward desire to preserve one's own genes. I won't go into the various feelings people experience when they are in love. There are literally mountains of literature written on this topic. What I do want to talk about though, is why people talk about love less frequently now. Why, perhaps fortunately, do we hear so rarely of the Laylas and Majnuns, the Romeos and Juliets, the great tragedies of unrequited love, and the murders and suicides inspired by love? There are two reasons, and both arise from the greater freedom of choice that exists in the world today.

The first reason is that people generally have a healthier ego, as we mentioned before. This prevents one person from totally losing themselves in another.

The second reason goes back to free love, which is also a consequence of freedom of choice.

In the past, normal sexual attraction experienced towards someone of the opposite sex who might have lived close by was often taken to be love. In years gone by, the 'forbidden' nature of sex only strengthened the illusion that what was being experienced was actually true love and this incited physical passion as well as fantasy and obsession, sometimes to the extent that the individual lost their mind.

Today, with a certain amount of free love available, as soon as the love-sick have the opportunity to lead a regular sex life (and not necessarily with the object of their desire), the passion they originally experienced so intensely all too often passes. Although this is not always the case! Love definitely exists in the form of a passion that a person experiences exclusively in relation to another.

The kind of love that is all-consuming, that a person will remember as the best thing that ever happened to them, irrespective of the agony that so often accompanies it, can no longer be explained by the Law of Gene Preservation alone, even if that law is founded in love.

Tell me, God, does the Law of Gene Preservation really require the exceptional level of discernment that can only be afforded by true love?"

"Not at all. I have to admit, that I neither ordained the phenomenon of love, nor did I foresee it. What do you think about love and the Law of Gene Preservation?"

"I think that of all the unimaginably rich diversity of relationships between men and women, love and free love must represent if not total opposites, then at least incompatible consequences of freedom of choice.

Indeed, if free love 'circumvents' the Law of Gene Preservation, is promiscuous and expands freedom of choice in relation to the object of its passion, then love consciously narrows freedom of choice to the one and only object of its passion. Perhaps that's why something similar to love exists in animals among wolves and swans for example.

To summarise our topic I can say conclusively that *gene preservation is impossible without the participation of the opposite sex. It sometimes requires a painful restriction in personal freedom of choice and sometimes leads to that truly dramatic development in the relationship between the sexes which we call love.*

The human thirst to preserve one's genes and the thirst for freedom of choice are like yin and yang, tightly woven like a tangle of snakes at the heart of one in love, devouring each other, complementing each other, penetrating each other.

It is only in countries where women are totally deprived of freedom of choice and serve men exclusively for the purpose of enabling them to pass on their genes that the drama, the battle between the free will of two separate individuals is absent. Yet, neither is there love!"

"Fabulous! Now I can tell you why I could not have foreseen the consequences. Freedom of choice has made the form of human relationships so varied, that I could not have foreseen the full diversity these relationships would take. Everything is much simpler for all other types of living matter. Answer me this. You said that the love of legend in all cultures of the world has become much rarer than it was. Could this kind of love disappear altogether?"

"No, never!

I'll answer you with the lines of the Russian poet Vladimir Vysotsky:

But you cannot drive away the insane,
They have already agreed to pay:
Any price - they would even risk their lives -
So not to cut, to keep instead
The magical invisible thread,
That is woven in between their souls..."

CONVERSATION 15. FREEDOM OF CHOICE AND ADULTERY. MARRIAGE AND DIVORCE. HUMAN CLONING

"God, let's talk today about marriage, divorce, extra-marital affairs and jealousy."

"We talked about this topic before when we discussed the Law of Gene Preservation."

"Yes, I know, but today I'd like to talk about these themes from the point of view of Freedom of Choice."

"That would be very interesting. To consider these themes from that point of view should make for a rich topic of conversation."

"Then I shall begin right away with the most important point.

In any close human relationship, be it a relationship between a married couple or romantic partners, a relationship between friends or relatives, an official relationship, ideological relationships within a party, relationships between members of a sports team or those serving together in the armed forces, *conflicts are inevitable and quick to develop due to the Freedom of Choice of those involved.*

Of all these kinds of relationships never is the conflict surrounding Freedom of Choice as dramatic, nor the rift so painful, as when it occurs in a marital or romantic relationship. Why? The answer is quite simple.

The Law of Gene Preservation looms invisibly over the romantic relationship, whether the individuals involved are aware of it or not. *The battle for freedom of choice, therefore, conflicts with the principle law of all living matter.*

From its very first day the marital relationship, consciously chosen by both partners for Gene Preservation, comes under the crossfire of their Freedom of Choice. At first, both partners are reluctant to compromise even over minor issues like their daily habits. What they fail to realise is that *every time one partner secures a small victory in an argument it backfires into a sense of inescapable defeat in the heart of the other.*

A huge amount has been written about the problems of marriage over the years, both in scientific works and in fiction, and psychologists have endlessly disputed the issues of matrimonial conflict, but really, it all simply boils down to *the battle between two different people's freedom of choice and the struggle of each to preserve their common gene.*

Despite the fact that both partners share the intuitive understanding that the marriage must be preserved, at least until the Law of Gene Preservation has been fully realised, i.e. the children have been parented into adulthood and are capable of living independently, *the two partners' freedom of choice frequently transforms the marriage into a battlefield* made up of differences in taste, habit and lifestyle preferences. The battle is restrained temporarily by the instinct for Gene Preservation for the sake of bringing up the couple's existing children. And if neither partner knows when to compromise, which is so essential to any marriage, the desire to pass on their genes is no longer enough to hold the couple together. The battle between the two partners' freedom of choice gradually becomes unbearable. The marriage falls apart and divorce follows, even if it was a marriage originally born of love.

Childless marriages fall apart more easily because the Law of Gene Preservation is not present to mitigate the antagonism that comes from the two partners' conflicting freedom of choice as they move further down the path towards divorce. As you can see, the main reason for divorce is freedom of choice, namely the desire of each partner to maintain maximum individual freedom and reluctance to sacrifice even a portion of their individual freedom for the sake of the other.

In countries that have a patriarchal way of life, where individual freedom of choice is more limited in general, and where freedom of choice among women is limited to the children and the kitchen, divorce rates are much lower."

"Do you think that this state of affairs is preferable?"

"It is not my intention to evaluate human choices, God, but I can see very clearly that these nations are also moving in the same direction as other countries, towards growth in individual levels of freedom of choice and, as a result, to higher divorce rates.

I should add though, God, that pursuit of uncompromising freedom of choice is not the only cause of divorce. The other cause has its root in free choice as well and it is, of course, adultery or extra-marital affairs. Freedom of choice causes husbands to remember that there are many other women in the world, and wives to remember that there are many other men. Why do couples cheat on each other? People invent a thousand excuses: my husband is this, my wife is that, she was a beautiful femme fatale, there was heavenly passion, it was simple curiosity, and many, many more.

The real answer though is very simple:

It is the centuries-long process of the emancipation of individual freedom of choice, in particular in the unconscious, instinctive choice of one's partner in gene preservation, that compels the individual (both he and she) to push the boundaries of their choices time and time again.

It would be wrong to think that extra-marital affairs result from a weak or uncommitted relationship between two partners. I have known quite a few cases, in which a married man whose wife is adorable, beautiful, a sex goddess with the sweetest nature, the perfect mother to his children etc., travels alone somewhere for a short break only to hit on the first woman he comes across, even if she is as ugly as nuclear fallout and as stupid as they come, simply to make the most of a forty-eight hour love affair. Naturally, I have seen wives act the same way too.

There's no point in trying to allocate blame, or determine the specific circumstances that lead to infidelity, when really one should acknowledge the role of the passions given by You, God, the passion to protect and pass on one's genes as well as the similarly powerful passion to assert individual freedom of choice to the maximum. Even curiosity about the opposite sex is really just a signal of the expansion of freedom of choice. Even Jesus Christ spoke through Matthew: *'whoever looks at a woman with lust hath committed adultery with her already in his heart.'*

In our previous discussions on this topic, God, we have pointed out that the Law of Gene Preservation nudges men, who are essentially polygamous by nature, into adultery (albeit subconsciously) by the fact of their instinctive need to sow their seed far and wide. Given the condition of today's society, we must admit that the Law of Freedom of Choice is also a factor that compels men and women to commit adultery. The freer society's norms become, the more tangibly the 'nudge' can be felt. We can see this happening in the West where attitudes towards adultery have changed hugely, becoming much more tolerant.

As an illustration, according to specialised research, the number of 'unfaithful' French men and French women has grown steadily, more than doubling over the past 40 years. Current statistics show that the number of 'unfaithful' partners has reached almost half in all married couples.

The most stable marriages in Western societies are those in which the partners mutually agree on the duties and responsibilities of each (not an easy task!) in the joint venture to preserve the common gene we call family.

The strength of the marriage bond in the 21st century is not what it was in the 20th century, nor was it then what it used to be in the 19th century. Moreover, the pattern of change the world over is quite definitely European.

The culture of tolerance in marriage developed as a necessary response to changing socio-economic patterns and issues of inheritance.

Today that culture no longer exists and the consequences are very evident. Divorce rates are growing throughout the world, and relatively quickly, not only in Western countries but in Asian countries that have chosen to follow the European development model. According to this model woman go out to work, have equal rights with men, are genuinely independent and consequently are equal to men in their assertion of individual freedom of choice.

No matter how many reasons for divorce sociologists document, global growth in the recognition of individual freedom of choice is the main underlying reason for all divorce. When you look at it more closely, the 'ideal marriage' of which most people (particularly women) dream is an illusion. In reality, one of the spouses usually totally crushes individual freedom of choice in the other, who complies with the oppression because they have lost themselves in their partner. I don't think I have ever seen a 'happy family' in which both partners are equally able to express individual freedom of choice.

For the same reason, 'strong marriages' can be observed in countries with totalitarian regimes or a totalitarian religion in which the country's citizens enjoy little or indeed no freedom of choice. In totalitarian countries such as Nazi Germany and the Communist Soviet Union, a divorced person of prominent social status might suffer a diminution in their future career opportunities. In countries where society's moral attitudes are determined by a totalitarian religion, any divorced person would be judged and rejected by the rest of society.

Even in some Old World countries, as little as half a century ago, securing a divorce was virtually impossible, which reminds me of the famous movie: *Divorce Italian Style.*"

"Do you want to take a break for a bit now?"

"No, I'm not tired. I am just getting warmed up! Let's continue. Let's move on to the theme of jealousy.

If you remember, we established the fact **that the Law of Gene Preservation is the source of jealousy**. Now though God, I want to add that in the light of freedom of choice, I see jealousy as a sin."

"You're right, it is a sin!"

"Despite the fact that it occurs in a person unconsciously, and is not of their will, jealousy is a sin because it represents an attack on another

person's freedom of choice, bestowed on them by You, by God himself. It's an attack on another person's soul and body even.

What is jealousy, God, if not a sin? It is not by chance that the words *jealousy* and *envy* are synonyms in English. They totally coincide in the French (*jalousie*) and Kazakh (*қызғаныш*) languages. Children should be taught from early childhood that jealousy is a sin, just as we teach them that feelings of envy and greed are sinful. After all, in the process of evolution people have managed to abandon the principle of 'an eye for an eye, a tooth for a tooth!'

There is nothing positive about jealousy at all. It is a totally destructive emotion. It destroys the person experiencing jealousy and alienates the object of their affections.

I have to admit though, God, that with regard to jealousy, humanity is changing for the better, showing greater respect for the lives of others and their freedom of choice. Just half a century ago, acts of jealousy were considered acts of valour. Murder committed out of jealousy was justified by the social morality of the time. In fact, that same social morality could drive a deceived husband to kill his cheating wife (more '*Divorce Italian Style*'). Fortunately, things have moved on somewhat since then."

"Have you finished?"

"No, but I am nearly there. From all that I have said above, God, I would not want to give the impression that all husbands and wives ever think about is adultery and divorce. No! People do not always suppress the gene preservation instinct and favour freedom of choice. A huge number of people who live first and foremost by the Law of Gene Preservation understand that a comfortable environment for bringing up children can only be created when the couple remain loyal to the family. There are still families held together by the true love that exists between man and wife.

God, I'd like to end today's conversation on that note, but I have a question which I hesitate to ask You."

"There should not be anything you feel you cannot ask me. Go ahead and ask!"

"It's about cloning."

"What is taboo about cloning? Plants have been cloned through vegetative propagation, bacteria and some species of lizard are naturally cloned, and the birth of monozygotic twins in animals and humans is also cloning."

"But, God, that is not really what I meant. I am talking about the artificial cloning of human beings. Is it possible to clone a real human being? Is cloning morally acceptable? Is man not usurping Your prerogative with technology? Should there continue to be a ban on human cloning as there is today in the laws of many states? And should cloning be considered an implementation of the Law of Gene Preservation or, on the contrary, its violation?"

"That's a lot of questions. Let's take them one at a time. The discovery of a technique that makes it possible to artificially clone a healthy human being is inevitable, and simply a matter of time. To be honest, when I gave man a means of procreation that involved a couple, I did not imagine that man would develop the technique of cloning so quickly, although having bestowed freedom of choice, I knew that sooner or later that time would come.

As far as whether it is morally acceptable or not, man is so driven by freedom of choice, since when has morality ever prevented man him doing anything? And what is morality anyway?

It was not so long ago that both divorce and abortion were an outrage morally condemned by society and yet today single-sex marriage is permitted. Cloning is not aimed at suppressing anyone's individual right to gene preservation or freedom of choice and so it cannot be considered a source of evil. Time will pass, and although problems connected with harmful mutations caused by repeated sequential cloning will remain an issue, the cloning technology will be made safe and then the ban will be removed.

There is no need to fear that cloning will conflict with the traditional means of gene preservation, even though it might appear initially that, unlike paired procreation, cloning gives one hundred percent gene preservation due to the absence in a child of the fifty percent gene makeup inherited from a second parent.

Love will remain on the Earth as well as the irresistible attraction to the opposite sex and, finally, children will still need both parents. And for those few who are unable to have a family for psycho-physical or other reasons, cloning will be the only way they can exercise their right to gene preservation. Do you understand?"

"Yes, God, I do! I suspect it will be partners of single-sex marriages who will welcome this opportunity most..."

"Perhaps..."

CONVERSATION 16. FREEDOM OF CHOICE AND THE UPBRINGING OF CHILDREN

"God, I'd like to return to the subject of raising children, which we discussed previously in the context of gene preservation. Knowing as I now do, that You bestow freedom of choice upon every child at birth, how does one explain the fact that parents constantly try to suppress their child's freedom of choice from its very early years, albeit in the name of saving and preserving their genes. For instance, forbidding a child to put its hand in the fire, cross the street in the wrong place, climb trees and so on."

"You are quite right to emphasise that a child is restrained in their 'early years' and the parents are quite right to do so! It is at this age that parents take upon themselves the responsibility of suppressing freedom of choice in their child because in doing so they are prioritising the Law of Gene Preservation."

"Unfortunately and sometimes even tragically, parents continue out of habit to suppress their child's freedom of choice when the child has reached adolescence. The parents dictate what clothes the child should wear, which friends they should have, which sport they should play, what profession they should choose, who they should marry and even the religious and political views to which they should adhere. When parents are unwise enough to have raised a child who is desperate to assert their freedom of choice and totally incapable of compromise, a tragic breakdown in the parent-child relationship is inevitable. A friend of mine who found himself in a situation like this in his youth once said: *The people I fear the most are those who are willing to give me the shirt off their back and in return demand my soul!*"

"He put it brilliantly. And I would agree with him."

"As far as I have observed, aside from habit there is another reason why parents turn into despots. I could never understand why some parents try so hard to look after their child's soul that they end up breaking their spirit, instilling by force the perfection they never achieved themselves. The Law of Gene Preservation does not require that. All that is necessary to fulfil the Law of Gene Preservation is that parents provide the conditions that will enable their children to go on and continue their parent's line.

Among animals, this task is limited to bringing up the young and protecting them from predators at an early age (from other predators if the species is itself a predator). It is the same for people, only because of the differences in the human 'herd', the offspring have to be provided with additional conditions that will enable them to survive: good health, an education or profession, as well as other survival skills such as manners, the ability to get along with other two-legged beings and all that we would call an upbringing, until such time as an independent soul has taken shape. But that's all!

So why do many parents go beyond that and continue to put pressure on their children? Well, there is a very simple explanation for this.

Parents who put pressure on their children are often frustrated individuals, desperate to fulfil their own ambitions through their children. They end up denying their children the space they need for the independent development of the soul, and individual freedom of choice, which I am convinced is a great sin.

My next question concerns the age at which parents should begin to relax their restraint on a child's freedom of choice, gradually returning the right that belongs to the child from birth, a gift bestowed upon the child by You, not by its parents?"

"It all depends on the child. There is no 'one size fits all' approach. It is important to begin as early as possible and, as you have rightly pointed out, to gradually allow the child elements of freedom they are capable of mastering. It is best not to delay the granting of full freedom of choice, taking into account, of course, the time and the environment in which the child is growing up."

"I have also noticed, God, that in my parent's time children were given almost total freedom of choice at the age of between 14 and 16 years old, whereas today young people are more likely to reach this point aged somewhere between 18 and 25. I also see that children in villages and on farms, who start participating in the work of their parents' livelihood at a relatively early age, are given freedom of choice earlier than other children in well-to-do families who live in the town.

I have another question. God, do you know how important it is when naming a child to choose a name the child will like when they reach an age of self-awareness? And did you know that parents don't always manage it? Why is it that in such an important choice in a person's life as the choice of their own name, a person has no freedom of choice? And tell me, God, what do You think of the tradition observed among several cultures, according to which a child is given several names at birth?"

"Is this a test or something?"

"Well, You often test me, God!"

"Ok, I'll answer you then. A child chooses one of those names when they reach adulthood. Parents who are wise enough to give their child several different names, irrespective of how it might be explained in the context of their religious or other traditions, are in fact more often than not subconsciously allowing their children freedom of choice with regard to their name in the future."

"Well done! That's right! Now for the serious questions. God, do you think parents ought to allow their children to be brought up by a third party, a youth organisation of some kind?"

"Absolutely not with the exception of parents who are completely incompetent or incapable. *The individual alone is responsible for the genes they have reproduced! No-one else. And if you like, assume that a parent carries this responsibility in my name and on my behalf!* I did not expect a question like that from you."

"It is a rhetorical question, of course. I wanted to tell You what childhood can be like under a totalitarian regime. As a person who was born and brought up in the Soviet Union, I have witnessed the entire mechanism of Pioneer and Komsomol organisations grooming people from childhood to become obedient slaves, unthinking robots of the state. I have to admit that the zombification process was very successful in the absence of any other alternative external information source. All primal human values and traditions were turned upside down.

We were for instance encouraged to inform on our own fathers if they did not agree with state ideology and to inform on one's parents was considered a form of heroism. The state instilled people with false moral values, such as super shyness, simply by suppressing any signs of individuality or originality in a child, nipping in the bud any doubt about the correctness of this one ideology that informed their 'happy' childhood. The Pioneer and Komsomol activists worked constantly to cultivate in us a willingness to give up our lives to protect their system and ideology, and yet it was presented to us as the need to protect the homeland.

The Pioneer and Komsomol organisations strove to keep the entire younger generation under a constant and watchful eye. They would invent various kinds of ideological games, hold evening parties and debates, at which the young people were only permitted to speak aloud those thoughts that were harmonious with the communist ideology. As soon as the children escaped from school, safely beyond its gates, they played completely different games, held very different conversations and sang entirely different songs.

Later I learned that our upbringing in the Pioneer and Komsomol organisations was no different to the upbringing of young people in the Hitler Youth organisation in Nazi Germany.

There are many totalitarian ideologies in the world, leftist, rightist, religious-fundamentalist, but the hallmark of the most dangerous among them is the fascist-communist component for it is this regime that usurps the education of youth from early childhood, squeezing parents out of their children's upbringing, depriving them of their sacred duty."

"Tell me then, why do they do this?"

"What do you mean, God, why? It is obviously so that they can strip young people of freedom of choice in early childhood and prevent them from learning that this, Your God-given gift exists! I have seen how schools in democratic countries prohibit all ideological propaganda, including religious propaganda."

"Yes, life was hard for you then..."

"It was the life You gave us, God. Although there are people for instance who are born and grow up in prisons and think that is how life should be and when they grow old they do not want any other kind of life."

"In response to your reproach, I should remind you that it was not I who gave you that life, who sent the communists with their Pioneers and Komsomols. *Since you have freedom of choice, you alone are responsible for the life you choose.*

It's not all that grim though. There is the Law of the Growth of Freedom of Choice which does not depend on the will of any particular individual, and you, I hope, will come to that in our forthcoming conversations. I almost found myself adding, 'with God's help'."

"And I was almost tempted to answer, 'May God's help be with you!'

God, I'd like to return to the topic of the Jewish phenomenon in the light of today's topic about raising children. We touched on it when we talked about the Jewish attitude to the Law of Gene Preservation. Now I'd like us to talk about the Jewish attitude to freedom of choice. Again, I don't know of any other nation that can boast such a high percentage of unblinkered, unbrainwashed individuals with such a diversity of individual opinions on almost any matter. These are people with a genuine interest in the opinions and cultures of others. In my view, this quality explains the huge role the Jews played in the development of the traditional cultures of Russia, France, Germany and the United States in the 19th and 20th centuries, and even earlier, in Spain.

And today we see their role in the development of world culture and science. They participate in all kinds of social movements and often appear on both sides of a social conflict. I believe that the reason for their sense of agency and the reason for their success lies in the freedom of choice Jewish families develop in their children.

As early as their teenage years, children are free to hold their own views on any issue, including politics, even if it differs from that of their parents' or, for that matter, the dominant view held in society.

The teaching of freedom of choice one sees in Jewish families is a continuation of the Law of Gene Preservation and life proves it. The approach of nurturing a free spirit in a child is today becoming increasingly widespread in all western societies, and especially in the US. In totalitarian countries, fearing for their child's life, parents teach their children to hide their opinions, and thereby cultivate a kind of hypocrisy in their children at an early age. Their fear is so strong, so deeply absorbed into flesh and blood, that in post-communist countries, where people are no longer shot or imprisoned for expressing their own opinions, parents from one generation to another, continue to cultivate this fear in their children, bringing into the world new generations of spiritual slaves. And these parents find the sole purpose of their life in gene preservation, as it is in the animal world."

"You're getting morose again..."

"I cannot forget my former life, a huge part of which I spent in the USSR. I know what I'm talking about. I'll finish there, but I do have one last question. Tell me, God, from what age does an individual start fighting for their freedom of choice?"

"The individual battle for freedom of choice begins in the cradle when the child resists being wrapped in nappies and ends with their death and the writing of one's will.

But of course, the intensity of the struggle is different for everyone."

"Thank you for your comprehensive answer, and goodbye."

"See you next time."

CONVERSATION 17. FREEDOM OF CHOICE.
SOUL AND MIND. MORALITY AND FALSE
MORALS. THE LIMITS OF MORALITY AND THE
LIMITS OF FREEDOM OF CHOICE. THE GENIUS,
THE CRIMINAL AND THE REVOLUTIONARY.
WHY WE LOVE OUR FRIENDS. YOU SHALL
NOT COVET YOUR NEIGHBOUR'S SOUL

"God, when it really comes down to it, what exactly is the soul?"

"I don't know."

"Recently, God, 'I don't know' seems to be Your answer to everything!"

"True! In our initial conversations, I explained that I had given all living beings the Law of Gene Preservation and that I also gave human beings the Law of Freedom of Choice. What the results of this have been, you probably know better than I do. This is why I encourage you to try and answer your own questions. For me, Earth is simply a grain of sand in the Universe. Believe me, I have enough on my plate besides worrying about what goes on down on Earth.

Anyway, we agreed last time that you would find the answer to this question yourself. I don't know any more than you do. You were supposed to be prepared."

"I did prepare, it is just that I did not find a straightforward definition despite the fact that a mountain of literature has been written about the soul, mostly by poets, philosophers and especially theologians. Christian representatives of the latter even went as far as to ask whether the soul existed in women at the famous

Macon Cathedral in 585 AD, where supporters of the existence of a soul in women took the majority with just one vote."

"And what conclusions have you arrived at?"

"I have no definition for the soul. Neither for my own nor for anyone else's! Similarly, we have no definition of the mind, but nonetheless, we confidently point to those who bear these notions distinguishing between the spiritual and the heartless, the clever and the stupid. I wonder whether the mind and soul emerged simultaneously with primitive man's first attempts to use Your gift of freedom of choice.

Learning the hard way from unsuccessful choices primitive humans experienced suffering which developed the mind. They experienced the greatest suffering when individual freedom of choice conflicted with the freedom of choice of another, and the conflict could not always be resolved by asserting one's physical superiority, particularly if the other person was from the same tribe or the same cave, i.e. one's kin. Then, as a result of man's observations and nascent ability to analyse, they began to suspect that the other participant in the conflict might also be suffering.

That's when people developed compassion, the first and clearest sign of the human soul which later became known as humanity. Some exhibited a lot of compassion, others less and some, none at all. We say of the latter that they 'have no soul.'

The human being who placed soul above all else and called the world to compassion was, as you know, the Prophet Jesus. Step by step, people began to understand, and then to respect the right of another person to their own freedom of choice. *And the more a person valued their individual freedom of choice, the more they respected it in others* as we can see happening in the West today."

"So tell me, what most of all affects the formation of the soul, or does it remain unchanged once it has emerged?"

"God, what a question! The soul is continually evolving over a person's life, from birth right up until the moment of their death. Each person's soul develops in its own way, depending on the degree of Freedom of Choice the individual has chosen for themselves every time they come up against the problem of choosing how to behave and how to react to the world around them. *And the greater the variety of choices a person considers, the greater their soul expands and develops. When a person acts solely according to instinct, it does not develop at all.*

Mostly though, people try to influence the souls of others, in other words, they try to change each other through conversation. Like for example you and I are doing."

"Hang on a moment! Are you saying that you're trying to influence me?"

"God forbid! Sorry, it just slipped out again! I feel so comfortable talking to You and I have got so used to You, that I sometimes forget who I am actually talking to. I am not so arrogant as to think that I would influence you. Nothing could be further from my mind. After every encounter with You my soul sings with happiness. I'm serious. As far as people are concerned though, that's all we ever do. We are always trying to influence each other's soul with our words, whether it is a request to our parents in childhood, our answers to exam questions at school or university, our responses during an interview with an employer, our part in an argument, or a declaration of love. Before you turned your back on him, the Kazakh poet Olzhas Suleimenov expressed the importance of words in the struggle to influence the human soul probably better than anyone:

Any moisture poured into a jug,
hurries to take on its cast form,
and the word, penetrating deep into the soul
strives to give it her own form.

Politicians and evangelists, in particular, strive to influence the souls of entire nations with their speeches and sermons. And among them there are many of whom one would have good reason to be wary. The 19th century Irish writer Oscar Wilde expressed the idea in his novel 'The Picture of Dorian Gray' that any attempt to influence another person's soul was quite immoral.

'Have you really a very bad influence, Lord Henry? As bad as Basil says?'

'There is no such thing as a good influence, Mr. Gray. All influence is immoral - immoral from the scientific point of view.'

'Why?'

'Because to influence a person is to give him one's own soul. He does not think his natural thoughts, or burn with his natural passions. His virtues are not real to him. His sins, if there are such things as sins, are borrowed. He becomes an echo of someone else's music, an actor of a part that has not been written for him. The aim of life is self-development. To realise one's nature perfectly - that is what each of us is here for. People are afraid of themselves, nowadays. They have forgotten the highest of all duties, the duty that one owes to one's self.'[6]

---

6 Wilde, Oscar. The Picture Of Dorian Gray. Penguin Classics (2006) ISBN 978-0-14-144203-7

"How interestingly this Wilde puts it. And what is your opinion on the matter?"

"I agree with him, only on the basis of a different principle. It is not for me to proclaim what is moral and what is immoral. But I do believe that *the soul, as the mirror of Your gift of freedom of choice, as its direct consequence, a person's ability to choose belongs to You and to You alone! And for this reason, no-one has a right to try and influence another person's soul. Except for You!*"

"I really like you!"

"But I'm serious. I really mean what I said. And many people across the world think the same way. There is a reason why the Kazakhs, the Russians, and many other peoples say of the deceased: '*They have given their soul to God.*' In days gone by Russian soldiers had a saying '*Give the soul to God, one's life to the fatherland, and one's honour to no-one!*'

I appreciate the fact that they made a clear distinction between the soul and the physical life.

I always wondered about the Russian expression used at a person's death: '*the soul has suffered its lot...*' and why at funerals they drink '*to the soul's repose.*' Now I understand that this can only be said of advanced souls, of people who have spent their entire life torn and languishing in search of choice. So what do you think of my little talk about the soul?"

"Not bad at all. I particularly liked the part where you said that the soul belongs to God, that is, to me. Had you finished?"

"Almost. I just want to finish with the call '*You shall not covet your neighbour's soul!*'

And with God's help, that is, Your help, I shall move on to the theme 'Morality.' God, do you have any opinions about morality?"

"Absolutely none whatsoever!"

"Fabulous! I was certain you'd say that! So why did they have to mess with my head since childhood, feeding me all sorts of morals my soul could not accept?"

"Who messed with your head?"

"First of all my parents, hammering the family morals into me as something indisputable, then the teacher at the Soviet school, also with the authoritative totalitarian morality of Marx, Lenin, and finally, the priests of endless different denominations, trying to convince me that their morality somehow came from You through revelations to some very 'dodgy' individuals. At the same time, I could see very clearly that *morality changed radically from one family to another*, that the morality of my street friends who, to put it mildly, did not get on very well with the juvenile courts did not correspond with morality as our school teacher explained it and that serious discrepancies existed between representatives of different confessional backgrounds, who often preached one kind of morality and lived by another.

I saw that *morality varies from person to person, from group to group, from nation to nation.*

And the most interesting thing is that when I began to study history, I realised that *morality changes with time. Morality will even shift to its exact opposite when the conditions that once produced it yield to change.*

When a new set of circumstances appears it is the people with a highly developed sense of individual freedom of choice that first try to change the status quo. More conservative individuals with a less developed sense of freedom resist change for as long as possible but give up in the end. Man always has freedom of choice, unlike other creatures, who only change their way of life when they are forced to by the natural environment.

Now I understand that the *morality which is said to be inherent in God*, or, as the atheists prefer to express it, in Nature, naively thinking that replacing the word 'God' with 'Nature' will make them sound more scientifically convincing, *does not exist at all!"*

"If you are going to continue talking about morality, you could at least start with a definition of the word!"

"That's easy. But first, a counter-question: *Are there limits to the gift of freedom of choice?"*

"No. None!"

"I'd agree with that but only up to the point where a person who does not like me has the freedom of choice to kill me".

"Don't forget that you have the freedom to choose to protect your life at any cost and by any means!"

"Well, God, now I can give a definition of morality. In brief, *morality is a set of rules aimed at limiting individual freedom of choice and these rules are chosen by the individual on a soul level to observe consciously and voluntarily. The rules dictate what is right and wrong, what is 'good' and what is 'bad' and are created so that people can get on with those around them.*

These limitations, God, are accepted as an indication of Your great mercy."

"Hang on a moment now! Don't rush ahead. I totally agree with your definition of morality but does it imply that man carries full responsibility for his choice of rules?"

"Absolutely!

That is why there is no single morality that can be observed by all. Every individual chooses their morality in accordance with the nature of their soul and their capacity to make choices. Any community will only exist for as long as its members adhere to the same basic moral values. If there is a conflict over moral values, the community will fall apart, whether it represents a family, a political party, a friendship or any other group of people in which the group's members have freedom of choice.

The most fundamental moral values which unite people in single nation-states, and even in the world community, are set out in constitutions and in the United Nations Universal Declaration of Human Rights. These documents essentially represent a set of limits placed on individual freedom of choice in relation to others.

For example, the right to life prohibits anyone from depriving another human being of life, no matter who they represent, an individual or a public authority. The only exception to this would be cases that have been specified by laws adopted by a country's majority population.

The right to equality, freedom of speech, freedom of movement, etc., all prohibit one individual from infringing upon another even partially in the enjoyment of these rights."

"Does everyone accept the laws of the state which have been established by the majority?"

"No, not all. Minority criminal worlds exist, which live by their own system of morality, according to which problems may be solved by violent means and killing is found acceptable. Most nations, in the form of the state, choose to defend their right to freedom by pursuing members of the criminal world, sometimes even destroying them. Within any nation-state, there are always groups emerging who whilst working within the framework of the constitutional rights would still encourage their members to assert a new kind of morality that either strengthens or relaxes established restrictions on individual freedom of choice.

The type of groups that strive to limit personal freedom include all kinds of religious fundamentalist organisations that restrict their followers in choice of clothing, diet, hairstyle, daily routine, working on Saturdays, etc., as well as groups of a fascist-communist persuasion who preach imperial ideas, delusions of the superiority of one race or class over another and lead to dictatorship.

The main threat totalitarian ideologies pose to Your divine gift of freedom of choice, God, is that they place a total restriction on freedom of personal conviction and belief, from which all free choice stems.

And then, God, there are those groups that seek constantly to loosen the restrictions placed by their communities on individual freedom of choice.

These are primarily creative communities made up of academics and artists. Such communities allow new scientific theories and artistic styles to shape their ethical values and these, in turn, form the fairly rigid framework within which the next generation must work. With time the 'new morality' exhausts itself and falls short of being able to explain emerging facts of nature, in the case of science, or of reflecting the aesthetic needs of the time, in the case of art.

And then there are certain people who don't seem to be affected by the limits the predominant 'morality' places on freedom of choice, and we call these people geniuses.

Geniuses are people who offer solutions to problems which go beyond the normal boundaries of existing conceptual frameworks and knowledge. Their revolutionary solutions usually meet initially with universal misunderstanding and even hostile rejection from others who are either unable or unwilling to go beyond normal perceptions.

Here is a textbook example from Physics at the beginning of the last century. In the atmosphere of crisis which hung over physics after the Michelson-Morley experiments, the great mathematician Henri Poincaré and the great physicist Hendrik Lorentz came very close to creating the special theory of relativity. The two scientists already had almost all the relevant equations and their consequences, and had set forth hypotheses to express the key ideas of relativity. Yet they still could not step beyond the framework of Newtonian mechanics. It was only the brilliant Albert Einstein who dared state that this was not just a hypothesis but a new physical, or if you like, divine reality, and that all the incredible physical consequences of the relevant equations actually occur in the material world. The subsequent creation of the general theory of relativity convincingly proved the authorship of the special theory of relativity.

I can't help but recall the saying of Arthur Schopenhauer on the difference between talent and genius: '*Talent hits a target no-one else can hit. Genius hits a target no-one else can see*'."

"I understand what you mean when you say that geniuses are people who think beyond the normal boundaries of freedom of choice. Are there other types of people who go beyond these norms?"

"Yes, God, there are! Criminals and revolutionaries! But there is a substantial difference between geniuses on the one hand and criminals and revolutionaries on the other.

Geniuses go beyond the normal limits in the theory of knowledge and the arts. Criminals and revolutionaries fail to recognise the normal limits of social morality, expressed in the state legal system.

There is also quite a difference between criminals and revolutionaries. *Criminals violate the law in secret, without infringing upon it directly, acting purely in self-interest. Revolutionaries act openly to overthrow the law, which they find unjust, and call the people to revolution in the interests of a large portion of the population.*

Given their historical experience, one would hope that the countries in the West, have finally learned to build public systems, which allow for revolutionary change to be made to outdated systems of legislation, thereby pre-empting the causes of violent revolution. One can see signs of this in the passing of laws on single-sex marriage and euthanasia that have recently become more universally accepted. These examples show that *morality varies not only in space but also in time.*"

"How exactly does 'morality change in time'?"

"Morality is part of man and it evolves over time just like the rest of humanity in accordance with Darwinian theory. If we said earlier that man's evolution depends on change in the natural environment, now we must include the level of freedom of choice in that environment as a factor for change, for it is on this that the condition of morality depends.

The higher the level of freedom of choice in society, the more liberal and humanistic that society's morality will be.

When the level of freedom of choice in society falls, its state of morality drops also, as we witnessed in 20th century Communist Russia and Nazi Germany, and in Mao Zedong's China and Pol Pot's Kampuchea. In these societies, the cruel destruction of millions of people led to widespread whistle blowing and the flourishing of general fear. The mass rejection of freedom of choice which followed served to benefit one or another ideological chimaera. Glory to thee, o God, that all these monsters were temporary and localised.

Finally, I'd like to end our lengthy conversation on morality, by looking at what might be the most wonderful example of freedom of choice - friendship. From early childhood, we start seeking out our friends and we find them among those with whom we have common moral values. It is to our friends that we reveal the most intimate corners of our soul, which we hide even from our closest relatives. Only our friends love us just the way we are, without trying to change us in the ways that our parents do, our husbands and wives and then our own children do. Friendship will gradually blossom into such devotion that a man will rush headlong into a bloody fight for the sake of a friend without stopping to weigh up the reason for the conflict or the consequences of joining it and he will do the same for the woman he loves.

The difference between friendship and love is that love is based on the instinct to preserve one's genes, whereas friendship is a pure product of freedom of choice."

"Have you finished?"

"Are you in a hurry?"

"No, carry on!"

"That is not quite all I wanted to say. I would like us to talk a little about false morality."

"And what about false 'morality'? Have you become a moralist now?"

"Goodness me, no. Nothing frightens me more than moralising. It's just I wanted to share an illustrative example of how people make up moral principles which not only have no substantial foundation but on the contrary, totally contradict Your laws. This is what I would call 'false morality.' Recently I heard a young man telling another that when he meets girls they start off by assuring him that they don't want to get married and prefer 'free love', but once you get to know them better, it turns out to be just the opposite. One has to wonder, who instilled the idea in these girls that the desire to get married and have children, that is, to fulfil the Law of Gene Preservation is somehow shameful, but having casual sex isn't?"

"Do you judge them?"

"No, not at all! I try not to judge anyone or anything. Aside from murder and encroachment on freedom of choice. With this one example I bring the topic of false morality to an end, otherwise, I fear I really will start moralising.

What's more, the Law of Freedom of Choice is slowly but surely freeing humanity from false morality. Not long ago, when I was young, it was unthinkable for a woman to give birth to a child out of wedlock because of the stigma surrounding illegitimacy. Today, in developed countries, where it is possible for a woman to raise a child alone, society no longer condemns single mothers and even welcomes the single woman, who, having reached a critical age, fulfils the Law of Gene Preservation and decides to have a child on her own.

People are beginning to understand that *the right to preserve one's genes and the right to freedom of choice are more important than any other concocted system of moral values and ethics."*

"Yes, that's an encouraging example. Shall we draw conclusions then from our conversation?"

"You are in a hurry, God, after all! I have taken up too much of Your time today, but not without good reason. I said once to one very invasive individual that *any life lasts for a finite period of time, and so when you encroach on someone else's time, you encroach on part of their life!*

Your life, God, is infinite in both directions on the arrow of time. You have always existed and you always will. Time for You is inexhaustible and so I have no qualms about taking up this part of Your life."

"Even so, let's conclude."

"What is there really to conclude, except that *the soul, manifest as the individual's capacity to choose, originates with You, God, whereas everything the soul chooses, including one's morality which places limits on free choice, originates with the individual?*

From the moment of birth to the very last breath, a person's morality exists in a constant state of collaboration not only with the morality of others but with the collective morality of society. Lucky is the individual whose personal morality harmoniously coexists with the collective. Life is far from easy for those whose personal sense of morality finds little room to breathe among the social group. Yet it is the individuals who succeed in broadening the framework of collective morality and shifting society even just a little way further along the arrow of time, who lead truly interesting, happy lives.

So, God, if my explanation of the difference between the soul and morality, and the origins of both is clear, I shall leave You today with a few lines by the Soviet poet Yuri Levitansky:

Everybody chooses for himself
His religion, loyalties and women.
Service to a prophet, or a demon,
Everybody chooses for himself.

Everybody chooses on his own
The word for loving and the word for praying.

*   *   *

I am choosing too - as best I know how.
Bearing no grudge against another,
Everybody chooses for himself."

CONVERSATION 18. FREEDOM OF CHOICE. EQUALITY AND SLAVERY. COLLECTIVISM AND EGOISM. REVOLUTIONS AND THEIR LEADERS.

"God, You create all people different, and yet you have said that we are all made equal. Wherein lies the equality you speak of and what is this thing that people have always dreamed of and of which many people around the world continue to dream?"

"Yes, I create people who are strong and people who are weak, some beautiful and others ugly, the noble and the ignoble, geniuses and idiots. I have not made people the same, but I have made them equal!"

"Nicely put. People have argued about what true equality means since time immemorial, and the debate shows no sign of reaching any conclusion. Wherein lies Your gift of equality?"

"Every human being has an equal right to gene preservation and freedom of choice, regardless of anything or anyone. This is your birthright. Do you understand?"

"I am beginning to. Does that mean that no one on Earth has any privileges over another when it comes to exercising these two rights? If I understand you correctly, God, the government of any advanced, developed society is obliged to pass the necessary laws to guarantee its population some control over the protection of these rights."

"Precisely!"

"Equality in these two rights only? Is that all equality boils down to? God, what was to stop you making people equal across the board? Wouldn't that have been spared us all our social problems and conflicts?"

"Equality in two laws is quite enough!

Equality in the right to gene preservation implies equality in the rights to life, labour, wages, education, housing, inviolability of property, transfer of inheritance, equal access to education for children etc., so to everything essential to preserving one's genes. Equality in the right to freedom of choice entails equality in the right to vote, the right to elect and be elected, freedom of movement, freedom to choose one's place of residence, the right to choose one's marriage partner, the right to choose one's friends and community in accordance with one's personal interests, the right to choose one's education and profession, the right to political and spiritual freedom, and so on.

That's all. Would you really want to make people equal in everything as the early communist-utopians dreamed? What would the world be like if people were equal in everything? Could a world like that exist if 'full equality' means to remove all incentive for personal development and expansion of personal freedom, and as a consequence, all social processes are stifled leading to the 'social death' of the human community, similar to the 'heat death' of the isolated, ideal Universe?

As a person who was born and brought up in a communist country, you know very well that the idea of absolute equality has never been manifested anywhere in the world, and that in practice, it actually transforms into the opposite: state-institutionalised inequality, terror and slavery."

"Yes, and this is a good moment to talk about slavery. Slavery was abolished long ago, throughout the world. No-one is bought or sold in chains anymore, and yet, tell me, God, why is it that one can hardly say of a significant portion of the global population that they are free to exercise their God-given right to freedom of choice? Why is that?"

"Well, firstly, it really is not that long ago that slavery was abolished. You see, I have lived longer than you, and I have observed man for longer than you. Your human-like ancestors first appeared on the planet Earth millions of years ago and, like all gregarious beings, they lived solely for the purpose of gene preservation. Can life in a herd really be called free?

I gave freedom of choice to man just two dozen or so thousand years ago. You can see the difference, can't you? Once endowed with freedom of choice, people were so frightened of using it that they quickly became submissive, even voluntarily becoming their leader's slaves. People have lived this way, hardly changing their slave mentality for most of the history of human existence.

It was only much later, little by little, that certain individuals learned to exercise freedom of choice initially to improve the working and living conditions of the tribe. They chose between a nomadic and a sedentary lifestyle; they chose which animals to tame, which plants to grow, whether to live in caves or build primitive dwellings. As such, the first civilisations of *homo eligenti* emerged.

Then man invented the first means of data transmission - writing, at which point knowledge and information could be transmitted not only from father to son, accumulated over one generation but also from grandfather and great-grandfather to grandchild, accumulated over several generations. The new means of transmitting information widened the circle of educated individuals, those who had much greater freedom of choice, and this accelerated the evolution of human civilisation. The distribution of writing and hence the number of people exercising freedom of choice grew in geometric progression, and consequently, there occurred accelerated growth in the rate of the development of human civilisation.

For example, in ancient Egypt, when only the priests and Pharaohs were literate, no significant change in lifestyle took place for more than a thousand years. During this time people ate almost exactly the same food, wore almost exactly the same clothes, lived in almost exactly the same kind of dwelling and held almost exactly the same conversations. In the middle ages, when another stratum of literate individuals appeared, noticeable changes took place within the period of just a century. In the 20th century when education became widely accessible change took place within about a decade. Now in the 21st century, thanks to the internet and developments in information technology, civilisation changes its image almost every year. I am talking now, of course, of the technical side of civilisation. But it is not just technical civilisation that has developed. *The development of the arts reflects the soul's incessant desire to search for the limits of freedom of choice*, and it is the arts in particular that determine these limits at every stage in the development of human society."

"Excuse me, God, what You are saying is very interesting but you have wandered off topic. I was asking you about slavery."

"Ok. Let's begin then by establishing the definition of a slave. Who in your opinion could be referred to as a slave?"

"In my view, a slave is someone who is totally deprived of freedom of choice.

Fortunately, there is now very little slavery in the world, of the kind by which a person is kept bound in chains and permitted only to do what their owner requires of them.

But if one takes slavery to mean the inability of an individual to fully realise their fundamental rights relating to gene preservation and freedom of choice, i.e. the right to live, to marry and create a family, to bear children, the right to housing, to education for their children, the right to elect and be elected, the right to freedom of movement, to vote, and to form or belong to political, cultural, sporting and professional associations, then this type of slavery is still very much alive in parts of the world where people have no protection from aggressive acts perpetrated either by the state or by others in this world who throw their weight around.

I was born and brought up in the USSR, so I know what I am talking about. You know, God, we lived under the leadership of the Communist Party with an ideology as 'beautiful' as Marxism-Leninism, which promised paradise on Earth to all who labour. How is it that this ideology turned into its opposite? Why did this happen?"

"Can you not guess?"

"No."

"Then think about the German Nazis, who also promised paradise on Earth, not to those who labour but to the 'Aryan race', and consider where that ideology eventually took the German people."

"I don't see any direct connection between Russian Communism and German Fascism. How are people to recognise when an ideology is dangerous? How do we protect ourselves? Enlighten me, God!"

"The connection is obvious. Both fascism and communism are quite open and honest in proclaiming not only the superiority of one race or one class over another but, most importantly, the absolute supremacy of the state over the individual. They warn their citizens in advance, equally as honestly, that any individual who steps out of line will be destroyed. Collectivist ideologies in the name of race, class or any other population group that advocate hatred towards other groups, fundamentally negate individual freedom - my gift to man.

Non-recognition of individual freedom of choice leads naturally to the circumstances in which a totalitarian ideology can come to power. The leaders who promised happiness to a certain race or class end up enslaving them instead and once they fear they might be losing their grip on power they will unreservedly destroy millions of human beings."

"God! How simple it all is in a way! I can see now that no party or state has the right to encroach on or limit the freedom of choice of any individual! Only our parents have the right to limit our freedom of choice and then, only in childhood for the purpose of protecting our young lives. When we become adults, it is only respect for the freedom of choice of other people that should ever limit our own personal freedom of choice. And these reciprocal restraints to personal freedom of choice should be agreed upon by the majority of the population and enforced by the legal system. Tell me God, in Your opinion, were communism and fascism inevitable from the point of view of history?"

"They were never my design, but they were, unfortunately, unavoidable. Communism and fascism revealed to the world what horrors result from the total public denial of freedom of choice. And I hope that people learned this terrible lesson once and for all and that similar ideologies will never be successful in coming to power again, anywhere in the world, at least in the parts of the world that are free."

"I must tell you a story, God, about the residual effects of a totalitarian ideology.

No less atrocious than the destruction of millions of people is the mentality of slavery, which was sown by the Communists in the souls those who live in most of the former Soviet Union.

Nobody is executed at gunpoint anymore for freely expressing their thoughts, and mass dissident concentration camps no longer exist, and yet people continue to experience fear verging on panic in response to any form of authority, even if they have done nothing to violate the law. They are even more afraid of public opinion. They are afraid to vote freely at elections even if no-one is standing behind them; for some reason, they automatically slow down when they spot a traffic control vehicle even if they are driving within the speed limit. In other words, they are afraid of their own shadow. Yet when there are no police in sight they boldly overtake other vehicles on the opposite side of the road, swear at other drivers, and chuck rubbish and spit out of the car window.

I call it the *freedom of the unfree*.

When the state publishes a law that people believe is unjust, they do not protest against the legislation; instead, they set about finding ways to evade it - to outwit the law.

Is this not a form of voluntary slavery?

I believe *that a person becomes a true slave not when their hands and feet are shackled with chains, but when they allow their soul to be chained and their freedom of choice to be obliterated.*

Spartacus was not a slave for a single minute of his life! Voluntary slaves can be found even in the free world, albeit much less frequently. Then there are other people who have been deeply affected by the conditioning of their upbringing that involved some kind of ideological propaganda. The conditioning might come from family, school, life on the street, a religion, party politics, and even the television. Sometimes these people are simply unable to break free of the influence of their conditioning and no longer know how to exercise personal freedom of choice, or perhaps they lose the desire to. Why do people change in this way, God?"

"Life is simpler that way!

It's hard to live in freedom, very hard, because you have to make your own decisions at every step of the way!

Still, what you and I must remember is that voluntary slavery, re-nunciation of personal freedom of choice, is still a matter of personal choice!"

"To hell with any kind of upbringing or education that leads to slavery!

The worst thing is that *slaves will always try to enslave others!*

I have noticed that *this is something people who have a free spirit never try to do!*"

"Never curse anyone or anything, human being!"

"Ok, God, I'll try. But I have to say, that in my life I have had dealings with various fallen people, even real criminals, but never has my contact with them been as chilling as when I have had to deal with people who have become voluntary slaves."

"It's not as bad as all that! I remember you mentioned something about a law, according to which freedom of choice is grow-ing in the world."

"Yes, I remember. Let's talk about that in our next conversation which will probably be our last on the topic of freedom of choice.

Right now I have another question for You. All major religions instil in people the idea of their individual unworthiness. They spread the idea that man is a 'slave of God', that nothing depends on the individual at all. Tell me honestly, is that really what You want, a group of slaves?"

"Me - slaves? If I needed slaves to follow me, why on Earth would I have given man the gift of freedom of choice?"

"Thank you. I knew that was what You would say! God, how much longer will the consequences of slavery continue to have an effect on Earth? I remember the faces of those who in the 1990s, in the USSR, came out into the squares of the cities to defend the natural birthright of individual freedom of choice; those who rebelled against communist dictatorship. They were the most beautiful faces I have ever seen in my life. Unfortunately, the communist heritage of slavery turned out to be so heavy and overwhelming that the flash of freedom quickly faded in most parts of the former Soviet Union. So, I'd like to ask you again, God. How long will the effects of slavery keep their hold on Earth?"

"Ok, I'll tell you what I have observed in human beings from here, since the moment they received the gift of freedom of choice.

Basically, the entire history of mankind, its movement along the arrow of time, is a departure from the condition of slavery and continues to be so to this day.

Fear of freedom of choice, fear of responsibility for one's decisions pushes a person towards voluntary slavery. There has never been a time when the weak did not feel the need for 'support in this uncertain world'."

"God, does man have a right to revolution in the struggle for freedom of choice? A right to violence?"

"You know, the kind of person who rises up in revolution for the sake of personal freedom of choice and the right to pass on and protect their genes, never asks and will never ask the likes of you and me, whether they have the right to do so or not. A person who rises up in revolution has not a shred of doubt that these indispensable rights were given to them at birth, they just don't know by whom. Believers will say that it was I who gave these rights to man. As far as violent rebellion is concerned..."

"Hang on a moment, God, may I continue this thought?"

"Go on then!"

"Historically speaking, violence was inevitable! It was inevitable at that level of freedom of choice and corresponding levels of the development of the human soul and morality. Today, society condemns any kind of violence, although unfortunately, violence continues to be prominent in most parts of the world. But thanks be to God, things move on, and there are states appearing in the world in which people are learning to resolve almost any issue without resorting to violence. These are, of course, the countries in the West, Japan and South Korea in which the highest levels of freedom of choice exist."

"Do you really believe that the West has built an ideal society in which there are no issues with freedom of choice?"

"No, God, of course not. The only place you'll find an ideal society unencumbered by issues of personal freedom is at the cemetery. I am not saying that the entire population of all the countries in the West has fully mastered the embodiment of individual freedom of choice. We are talking about a minority, a third, perhaps even a quarter of the population only, but this was enough to make up a 'critical mass' and so even as a minority, this portion of the population was instrumental in building a society which provides the greatest possible freedom and equality to all its members. The current attitude to personal freedom of choice in the West is far from ideal, but at least there the development process is unfolding without bloodshed or violent revolution.

Unfortunately, you can't say the same of the rest of the world. In many other countries, the percentage of people who exercise freedom of choice is too small to exert any significant influence on the society in which they live.

People in the West have become so used to their European values and liberal morality, that many condemn outright the bloody violence of the very revolutions which ensured their country the level of freedom it enjoys today.

I remember a scene from a French film in which Robespierre sends Danton to the guillotine and is horrified by the terror that has been unleashed by the revolution. But then a boy enters the room, the son of a maid, who is reading aloud the first articles of the Declaration of human and civil rights, which he is trying to learn by heart: all human beings are born equal, power comes from the people, etc. These are the articles which for the very first time in human history, assert man's equal rights to freedom of choice and which are today incorporated into most of the world's constitutions.

It would be interesting to see where France, England and the rest of the world would be now if it hadn't been for the Robespierres and Cromwells of this world. Anyway, around the mid-20th century, various prophets appeared who called for the battle for liberty to be fought without violence, and without the total annihilation of evil forces resistant to change."

"And what was the outcome?"

"Well, You can see for yourself. Compare what Lenin and Stalin, Hitler and Mao Zedong were able to achieve, with what was accomplished by Mahatma Gandhi, Martin Luther King and Nelson Mandela!"

"Yes! *You can't force happiness on people by encroaching on their freedom of choice.*"

"I'd like to share another observation with you, God. Throughout the history of mankind, people have escaped from slavery because they have had the leadership of a genius; in the hour of revolution, the people will follow their leader. In the past, there has always been a need for 'leaderism', whereas today people are less dependent on an infallible leadership figure. In the protest movements of the West and in the most recent wave of revolutions - the Arab spring, the movement in the Ukraine and the protest marches in Russia - we no longer see the charismatic popular leaders of the past. Why is that, God?"

"I can see by the look on your face that you'd like to answer that question yourself."

"It's true. I would, because I now understand why. It's not that fewer charismatic personalities are being born into the world. It's that Your great gift of freedom of choice is slowly but surely doing its work! More and more people in the world are becoming conscious of the fact that they are free to make choices, and more and more people are beginning to exercise their own free will.

Fewer people want to lose themselves in another, whether that be a revolutionary, political or spiritual leader, the one they love, a friend, a literary figure, a film star or pop idol. One can only welcome the type of parent who raises their children to be immune to idolatry, who rather than teaching their children to bow their heads to leaders, encourages them to become leaders of their own lives. Both Moses and Muhammad warned against idolatry.

One of the visible consequences of the expanding scope of personal freedom on the planet is that the collectivist mentality, which has formerly played a huge role in humanity's survival, is gradually being replaced by an individualist mentality, a certain healthy egoism. In the West, where individualism has gained the upper hand, we see maximum observance of human rights, examples of broad-mindedness and fewer examples of xenophobia, racism and religious intolerance as a result.

Only a person who exercises personal freedom of choice and vigilantly guards their individual rights and liberty can truly appreciate and respect another person's right to freedom of choice.

God, let's return to the topic with which we began our conversation today - equality."

"Ok."

"Am I right in thinking that You create people equal only in their right to fulfil the two laws we have discussed, but different in all other ways?"

"Exactly!"

"So what about the peoples of the world? Do you also create them different like You create individuals to be different?"

"No! Absolutely not! All the peoples of the world are equal in every way!"

"So why it is then that different peoples live such different lifestyles? Why are some nations currently experiencing a stage of development that other nations completed much earlier in their history?"

"The nations of the world are like children from the same family who were born at different times. And sometimes it happens that the younger child catches up with their older siblings and even surpasses them."

"God, does that include the Jews?"

"Yes, they too are exactly the same! It is just that the Jews achieved awareness of the Law of Gene Preservation and the Law of Freedom of Choice earlier than any other nation. That's how they were able to escape Egyptian slavery and push further ahead along the arrow of time than any other people."

"I see. You mentioned different nations in the context of the arrow of time. I'd like to add something to what You have said about that, if that's alright."

"No problem!"

"I have lived in many different countries and have made what I think to be quite an interesting observation. Before I describe what that is, it would be helpful to think of different countries in terms of belonging to one of three tiered categories.

The first tier designates countries of the so-called western world and certain Asian countries which are following a European pattern of development. These nations stand ahead of others on the arrow of time and their cultural, technological and social development appears to be free of any noticeable influence from the rest of the world. Of course, these countries have a pluralised society made up of some groups which are more 'advanced' and others that are 'catching up.' Despite that, the divide between these two groups does not represent a hostile, or insurmountable obstacle. Society is free of intense, internal stress and so its problems and challenges which arise naturally as a product of the evolutionary process are dealt with organically, as they arise. First, an issue appears in the free press, then it is discussed across larger social groups until finally it is debated in parliament and government offices at which point the solution or chosen path ahead is encapsulated in the form of new laws.

The third tier is made up of tribes, who live pretty much isolated from the rest of the world. There are very few places left like this in the world today, with the exception of the jungles of the Amazon delta and some areas of Africa. Like the nations of the first tier, a lack of intense internal social pressure and major external influence is characteristic of the pattern of tribal development. The tribal community tends to evolve together, and similarly to the primitive peoples of the ancient past, it develops in accordance with the group's internal rules and laws.

That brings us to the second tier which is the largest of all. With minor exceptions, this tier is made up of the open countries of Africa, Latin America, the former Soviet Union and Asia. Here we can see examples of the more 'advanced' groups of these nations who live in large towns and cities, receive a western education, read western books, newspapers and magazines and listen to western music. They watch western television and cinema and most importantly, they know how to use the internet and so are observing 'live' the activities carried out by western democratic institutions for the observance and preservation of the right to freedom of choice.

These groups live on the ideas and concepts of Western 21st century society. On the other hand, in these second-tier countries, there is also a huge 'catch-up' population group, especially in the provinces, the members of which who do not enjoy the benefits we've just mentioned. This population group lag behind economic development in the rest of the country and continue to live by fundamentalist, religious or communist ideas that limit the level of individual freedom of choice to what it was at the beginning of 20th century. One could say that the nations of the second tier are 'stretched' along the arrow of time, contemporary 'advanced' and 'catch-up' population groups extending across a divide of more than a century. This explains the colossal tension that exists in these second-tier societies, and generally speaking the frequent outbreaks of civil war and revolution which wrack these countries occur when that inner tension reaches boiling point. Not surprisingly, the dictators in power exploit the chasm pitting the 'catch-up' group against the 'advanced' group.

Will the chasm that exists between groups in the second tier last forever, God? Will it continue to prop up authoritarian regimes serving as a source of inner conflict? Today, with the development of communications and population mobility these groups are no longer as isolated as they once were, which only goes to increase the probability of conflict between them."

"Things aren't as bad as they might seem! You mentioned a 21st century means of communication that is fundamentally different to anything we have seen before! It is a tool that provides virtually all segments of the world's population equal access to information and is intended to minimise the social divide that you've been talking about. This communication medium is called..."

"The internet! Why didn't I see it straight away! Pope Francis called the internet a gift from God for good reason! How very timely are Your gifts to man!"

"And on that up note, as you say, we will finish our conversation for today."

CONVERSATION 19. FREEDOM OF CHOICE, SUICIDE AND EUTHANASIA

"I would have preferred it if we could have avoided today's topic of conversation, God, but I can see that if we are going to continue discussing freedom of choice, that won't be possible. The topic is suicide and euthanasia. Let's start by discussing the animal world and the examples in our first conversation in which humans and other creatures sacrifice their own life for the sake of reproduction and the survival of their offspring. Can these be considered a type of suicide?"

"Of course not! The examples we were looking at illustrate the Law of Gene Preservation in practice, but nothing more than that."

"Then in Chingiz Aitmatov's novel, 'Spotted Dog Running at the Edge of the Sea', the three adults who took their lives to save one little boy did not commit suicide? Their deaths took the form of suicide but only by necessity as part of the fulfilment of the Law of Gene Preservation?"

"Precisely!"

"Ok, God, but what about known cases of self-sacrifice among many pack and herd type animals and even insects for the sake of the pack as a whole? For example, the pea louse has the facility to self-explode, sacrificing its own life to protect same species individuals from predators."

"We talked about this in our third conversation, referring then to this phenomenon as the species preservation instinct which is an extension of the Law of Gene Preservation. We also agreed that this instinct exists in people, and that we quite rightly refer to self-sacrifice for the sake of others as heroism."

"But there are also cases of 'voluntary' animal deaths, sometimes involving whole groups, that are not motivated by the instinct to save offspring or individuals of the same species. Whales, for example, will 'voluntarily' beach themselves on the shore."

"What do the scientists write about this phenomenon?"

"They explain that the cause lies in various mental disorders resulting from severe stress, similar to that experienced in humans. Mass voluntary death among whales is thought to be explained by man-made causes or by the motivation on behalf of diseased whales to free up habitat for healthy relatives. So, God, if this isn't suicide either, what exactly is suicide?"

"Suicide is the choice a person makes to end their own life. Only a human being has the faculty to make this choice.

When a person chooses to commit suicide they eliminate the possibility of any further act of choice. In other words, suicide is the direct killing of individual freedom of choice. If this choice is made by a young, childless individual, it also represents the termination of their right to gene preservation. What a tragedy for that person's family! This is why suicide has been considered a huge tragedy among all nations and a great sin in most religions. Do you know what the reason is, that most often drives a person to suicide?"

"I prepared for our conversation, God, and looked up the global statistics which clearly show that suicide has its roots in social issues. Be that as it may, I want to emphasise that, however paradoxical it may seem, every person who commits suicide experiences a sense of loss or fear of the inevitable loss of Freedom of Choice.

Most tragic of all are teenage suicides, which occur when, through ignorance and lack of life experience, a young person feels that the conflict they are suffering at school or at home is the end of the world. A young person may have thoughts of suicide when they feel driven into a corner, that they have no way out, that no other manoeuvre is open to them, and that they have no freedom of choice. In post-Soviet countries, the totalitarian system of raising and educating children is largely based on the principle of punishment and social disgrace and this system is a huge contributor to the cause of teenage suicide. We inherited this system of education from the Soviet school, when, for example, teachers would stand on duty at the school gate with a ruler in hand measuring the length of the girls' skirts or the length of the boys' hair as they were arriving in the morning.

No less a factor in cases of teenage suicide is the traditional patriarchal style of upbringing in families where children have no contact with their parents and priority is placed on 'avoiding bringing dishonour to the family.' Unfortunately, there are parents to whom, God, you have given children but not reason. The temporary right You give parents to limit their child's freedom of choice for the sole purpose of protecting that child until they reach adulthood is interpreted by some parents as the right to be master of their child's soul. Some parents so suffocate their children and their children's ability to make choices, that the child feels suicide is their only way out. It is true when they say: '*The road to hell is paved with good intentions.*'

No less tragically, another cause of suicide among young people is a lack of preparedness for adult life, the inability to handle the blows of unrequited love or exam failure and fear of the future.

Young men and women, who are socially and mentally unprepared for adult life have no idea that the path that lies ahead of them will be filled with new loves, new friends, opportunities for travel, as well as professional and career related successes. Having experienced a profound loss of freedom of choice they carry out one final, fateful, irreversible act of will.

I think the reason why the statistics for male suicides are several times higher than the suicide rate for women can be explained by the greater sense of responsibility women feel towards their children, that is, the Law of Gene Preservation.

I suspect that the statistics for rural suicides exceed those for the city because life in the city tends to give greater scope for freedom of choice than in rural areas and so feelings of hopelessness in response to difficult situations may be experienced less intensely in towns than in the villages.

Of course, there are many other causes of suicide but, as I said earlier, to one degree or another, they are all connected to loss of freedom of choice or the fear of losing freedom of choice, for instance, as a result of serious illness and the subsequent inability to work, the loss of a much-loved husband or wife, loss of work in middle age, bankruptcy and fear of poverty, loss of social status and fear of prison confinement.

Did you know that in all countries across the globe, prison confinement, which is tantamount to the elimination of freedom of choice, represents the main form of criminal punishment?

But life is never straightforward! When freedom of choice comes out of the blue to people who have been used to living and working according to a strict schedule and strictly defined rules, they often feel as if they have lost their freedom. The risk of suicide is statistically proven to be higher among 'young' retirees, demobilised officers and long-serving inmates after their release from prison.

I won't go into other reasons for suicide here such as alcohol and drug abuse and psychological illness as these go beyond the topic of our conversation. I'd like to finish on this sad topic, God, by asking you one final question. Why have people resisted euthanasia for so long? Why is the ban on euthanasia being lifted only now in countries with characteristically high levels of freedom of choice?"

"Reverence for the Law of Gene Preservation has instilled in humanity the highest respect for the value of human life. Resistance to euthanasia is a kind of latent resistance to suicide. Gradually though, people are beginning to understand that an elderly person who is terminally ill is no longer connected to life in any way, and that when a person suffers horribly we must respect their last wish and assist them in carrying out their final act of choice. As you can see, here too, in this sad example, the degree of individual freedom of choice is growing!"

"Thank You, God. You have an answer to almost any question!"

"Why 'almost any'?!"

"Well, You could not answer my question about love."

"And it is a wonderful thing that I have not answered that particular question. Would people have written books, made films and put on plays dedicated to the theme of love if I had simply explained to you exactly what love is? Would people have composed music on the theme? How would they have lived even? Think about it! Goodbye!"

CONVERSATION 20. THE LAW OF HUMANDYNAMICS AS THE MAIN DRIVING FORCE FOR THE EVOLUTION OF MANKIND

"Hello, God! Today will be our last conversation on freedom of choice, and so we should finish by summing up our comments."

"I can tell that you have prepared for this conversation and have a summary ready."

"It's true, I do have and I would like to start our conversation with a summarisation. God, do you know about the Second law of thermodynamics?"

"?!"

"Sorry, I've done it again. I forget that all the laws of living and non-living matter function solely thanks to You. And still, I shall set forth this law as we are accustomed to doing so on Earth: the total entropy of an isolated system always increases over time. Now comes the good bit!

The Law of Humandynamics: Freedom of Choice on Earth always increases over time."

"Could you explain in a little more detail?"

"Yes. In physics, entropy is defined as the measure of disorder within a system: the less the elements of a system are subject to order, the greater the entropy. By analogy we may take the freedom of choice of a social system to be the measure of disorder inherent in that system: the less the people (elements) of a system are subject to any strict order, the greater the level of freedom of choice.

Primitive society, which began life in accordance with the Law of Gene Preservation alone, and was organised according to a rigid structure, similar to that of bees and ants, had the lowest level of freedom of choice. With time, freedom of choice began to eat away at society's rigid order and increased like the entropy of an ensemble of particles in statistical physics.

I am sure You will agree, God, if I say that currently, total freedom of choice on Earth is incomparably higher than ever before in the history of humanity. Slavery has been prohibited everywhere for a long time now. Racism is disappearing as a thing of the past. Growth in freedom of choice enabled the Americans to elect a black president for the first time. There is a noticeable decrease in discrimination against women. We see increasing tolerance towards religious, sexual and other minorities, who bear no threat to society. Around the world, most people, as least formally, have basic human rights: freedom to vote, freedom of movement, free elections etc., and even the right to fulfil the Law of Gene Preservation, which in the European convention is now referred to as the right to marry.

More recently, one country after another has recognised euthanasia as the human right to one last, tragic expression of freedom of choice!

The significant increase in tolerance, particularly in Western society, that has been witnessed over the past half-century is also a consequence of the Law of Humandynamics. In accordance with this law, all nations, irrespective of fierce resistance on behalf of the ruling regime, tend towards a Western-style democracy.

Increased freedom of choice has also influenced historical forms of how the Law of Gene Preservation is fulfilled. For example, there are ever fewer places left in the world where a bride can be forced into an arranged marriage. Recently, the British magazine The Economist[7] published an extensive set of statistics indicating that, according to the UN and the OECD, the portion of forced and arranged marriages in girls under 15 years of age has fallen throughout the world from 12% in 1985 to 8% in 2010. In general, in the countries of Asia and Africa the portion of arranged marriages has fallen from 72% at the beginning of the 20th century, to 40%, and in countries like China, Japan and Indonesia arranged marriages have all but disappeared. The education of women has obviously had a lot to do with the recent change which has inevitably entailed greater freedom of choice among women in society generally. Finally, barriers to inter-caste marriages in India are shown to be crumbling.

Now not only in the West but throughout the world, people prefer to plan their family and prefer to offer their children a good upbringing in terms of nutrition, health and education than to give birth to a large number of children. Global birth rates have fallen by half, from 5 children to one mother in 1960, to 2.5 children to one woman in more recent years.

We could talk forever about the growth of freedom of choice over the course of history and how freedoms have changed the face of society. Our entire history is a continual example of the influence of growing freedom of choice."

"And yet, wherever you look, there are cases where the Law of Humandynamics seems not to work, aren't there?"

"For instance?"

---

7 Smaller, smarter families. *The Economist*. [Internet] 23 January 2016. http://www.economist.com/news/special-report/21688585-love-and-marriage-have-become-more-individualised-smaller-smarter-families.

"Well, for instance in 20th century Communist Russia and Nazi Germany the level of individual and total freedom of choice fell sharply as a result of the coming to power of Communist and Nazi totalitarian regimes."

"Yes, that's true, it did, but firstly, neither Russia not Germany can account for the entire planet. They are simply a local part. And secondly, these were temporary phenomena. In physics temporary decrease in entropy in the local volume of a system of particles is called fluctuation. A fluctuation can last for a period of time if you isolate it from the remaining part. In confirmation of what I have said, it has been observed that after the borders of a totalitarian state are re-opened, people will immediately start crossing the borders increasing the overall level of freedom of choice for all mankind, in the same manner that was illustrated in the well-known physics experiment involving two different gases. The molecules of both gases were separated by a partition. As soon as the partition between them was removed, the molecules began to penetrate both sides of the space increasing the entropy of the entire system.

Once again, by analogy with the Second law of thermodynamics one may assume that the larger the country the more difficult it is to maintain a state of fluctuation with a low level of freedom of choice in comparison to the surrounding world. On the other hand, no matter how small a country, the probability of maintaining a state of fluctuation with reduced freedom of choice will tend to zero over time. For example, there is no doubt that the totalitarian regime of North Korea will eventually fall, in accordance with the Law of Humandynamics.

Abraham Lincoln clearly had an intuitive understanding of this law when he said: '*You can fool all the people some of the time, and some*

of the people all the time, but you cannot fool all the people all the time.'
Are you happy with my answer?"

"Very! Your examples are clear. Do you have others?"

"Yes, heaps! But that is not what concerns me. God, you know what happens, don't You, when the growth of entropy in an isolated system comes to an end?"

"Absolutely! Heat death. It's the final state of any closed thermodynamic system in which all energy types are transferred into the energy of heat movement which distributes evenly throughout the entire system. It's when the thermodynamic entropy of the system reaches its maximum. At this point, all the system's thermodynamic processes are exhausted reaching what is called the heat-death of the Universe."

"So, if we take the analogy of the Second law of thermodynamics further, it would mean that when the growth of freedom of choice reaches its maximum on Earth the next stage would be the "evolutionary death" of society in the system Earth?"

"Well, firstly, this is not going to happen for a very long time and secondly, whoever said that by that time the Earth would still be an isolated system?"

"How cunning You are, Creator! You have thought of everything!"

"Did you think it could be otherwise?"

"God, tell me honestly, did you know about the Law of Humandynamics before we started talking about it today?"

"Surely you haven't forgotten who is behind all fundamental laws of nature?"

"I used to think, that history had found a severe way of punishing the communists and fascists for trying to undermine the Law of Humandynamics. Now, I know who is responsible."

"If you are hinting at me, then you are quite wrong! I do not punish anyone. It is the laws that 'punish' and as you have rightly pointed out, *sooner or later, the Law of Humandynamics will sweep away all those who stand in the way of freedom of choice.*

And I agree with you; sooner or later, the workings of this law will sweep away the political regime in North Korea, but I repeat, that I have not interfered in the evolution of man or nature for a long time now, and have given over to the workings of the fundamental laws of the development of animate and inanimate matter, most of which you have already discovered.

Now that we are concluding our conversations on the topic of the Law of Freedom of Choice, I would be interested to know, as with the Law of Gene Preservation, how people perceive the Law of Freedom of Choice and what they feel about it?"

"Well, God, unlike the Law of Gene Preservation, I cannot say that people follow the Law of Freedom of Choice confidently and en masse. The thing is that one person's attempt to use the gift of freedom, often comes up against the freedom of choice of other members of society, who are in most cases more powerful, and this naturally gives rise to fear.

As You said yourself, God, the Law of Freedom of Choice is relatively recent, so a large portion of the world's population still has not achieved the general balance of liberty for all individual members and segments of society that we refer to as democracy.

Eventually, though, all nations will come to establish democracy because the Law of Humandynamics will leave them no other choice.

Having said that, whether they are consciously aware of it or not, every individual follows the Law of Freedom of Choice and does what they can to extend the scope of freedom of choice both for themselves and for their children. Don't good schooling and a decent university education give a person greater freedom of choice, like winning a competition or contest, or being promoted, receiving an increase in salary or developing one's business? This is why people celebrate so joyfully with friends and family each significant step on their path through life. What are these events if not celebrations of the Law of Freedom of Choice?! Many nations celebrate as public holidays the dates that mark the revolutions that won them independence or brought them democracy, in other words, that gave them a higher level of Freedom of Choice.

The desire for wealth is an intuitive striving for greater personal freedom. Yet without ardent, consistent work on a soul level, the 'freedom of choice' that wealth brings will remain nothing more than an illusion, for after satisfying the flesh, a weak soul is left with no choice at all. As You can see, God, we human beings also see the Law of Freedom of Choice as an expression of Your grace.

After one of our earlier conversations, God, I was left wondering why patriotism is diminishing in the modern world. Now I think I can answer that question. As freedom of choice becomes more widespread, contemporary societies are becoming more open, the West first and foremost. The world's common language (English) is growing in usage as never before. Knowledge of English creates excellent opportunities for travel, exchange in human resources, science, the arts and technology and active cultural borrowing of elements of fashion and national cuisine. Finally, in the context of the internet, an amazing technology that is unifying the entire planet, the motivations for patriotism are gradually becoming outmoded. It is not surprising, that the youth of today gaze at their 'educators' with genuine bewilderment when they encounter elements of a strong patriotic education.

Nonetheless, when a country is suddenly faced with an act of external aggression, surges of patriotic feeling can still be witnessed, even in democratic countries. National pride, however, is most alive and flourishing in authoritarian and totalitarian countries. Fearing the failure of their inevitably doomed political policies, dictators try desperately to keep a grip on infinite power by zombifying the country's population with xenophobic patriotism and hatred for the rest of the world.

When the world reaches a point of total globalisation, which it inevitably will do, as an effect of the Law of Humandynamics, patriotism will either disappear altogether or simply be reduced to the club-based patriotism characteristic of football fans.

Science has not yet confirmed the existence of hostile extra-terrestrial civilisations, which could potentially evoke a global patriotic response from the world's population, unless You happen to know whether such civilisations exist? If I know You though, You would not say, even if You did know."

"That's true. I would not say. Is that everything you wanted to convey about the Law of Humandynamics?"

"There is just one last comment I'd like to make, God."

"What is that?"

"The true value of any scientific theory, and of any law of nature, lies not so much in the explanation of existing phenomena as in the forecasting of new ones."

"Elucidate!"

"Well, God, for instance, I predicted that more and more countries would legalise euthanasia long before it started to happen. Now I predict that all bans on human cloning will be lifted."

"On what do you base your prediction?"

"On the notion that anything which stops short of impinging on the right to gene preservation and freedom of choice will at some point be permitted!

I am certain that many things will change in the life of man. Rituals and customs will change, including the traditional form of the institution of marriage, and many values will be reconsidered. Only the two most fundamental values - Your gifts to mankind - will remain unchanged: the inconsumable passion for gene preservation and expansion of the scope of individual freedom of choice.

With that, God, I conclude all my questions about the functioning of the Law of Freedom of Choice in man and the Law of Humandynamics in society and suggest that we progress to the main and final part of our dialogue."

"Ok!"

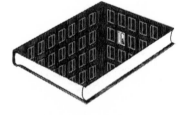

"I will not follow any one religion.
When I grow up, I shall make up my own."

From the statement of a teenage girl
in response to "The Last Faith"

PART III
THE LAST FAITH

CONVERSATION 21. GOD AND THE UNIVERSE

"Hello, God! What will we talk about today?"

"I want to ask you what you know about the Universe."

"Pretty much everything! Not me personally of course, but scientists. It all started with a Big Bang. Then everything started to move and evolve in accordance with Your laws which were discovered by Galileo, Newton, Einstein and Darwin..."

"'Discovered' is just the right word! Who do you think invented and initiated the working of these laws? Do you think it was easy for me to make all 'your' laws works harmoniously together so that they would never malfunction anywhere? Do you think it was easy to come up with all that and work everything out so that all your scientists had to do was 'discover' the laws of the Universe? I'm constantly afraid that someday, somewhere, one of the laws will fail."

"God, can You influence things at all? For instance, could you consciously contradict of one of Your own laws and stop it functioning as it should, even just a little bit?"

"That's the thing. No! Not even a tiny bit! If I were to destroy the natural workings of a single universal law, 'even just a little bit', then I would have to destroy it all!

Take this example. Imagine that the engines gave out on a plane whilst it was in the air. Even if a person extremely close to my heart was sitting in that plane, I still would not do anything about it. To my huge sorrow, the plane would fall from the sky in accordance with the law which Newton discovered and crash in the exact place and at the exact moment in time that even a schoolboy would be capable of calculating.

You see?"

"Yes, God, I do! Then let me ask You another question: When we studied physics at school, they were always talking about inanimate bodies. Tell me, God, as part of the Universe, is animate matter also subject to the laws of Galileo, Newton and Einstein?"

"Yes, of course! For instance, if you were to be thrown out of the window of a multi-story building, you would fall through the air like a stone, thrown out of the same window, at the same speed and along the same trajectory. You see?"

"Yes, that's not difficult to understand, it's just that Your examples are a bit..."

"Ah, well, you have to talk to a man in his own language. At least my examples are easy to understand!"

"God, I've thought of another question about animate matter. Since You created the first living cell and have been controlling the development of all animate matter on Earth..."

"What do you mean controlling? I don't control anything. Do you think I have nothing better to do than look after You lot? All I did was give the cell the Law of Gene Preservation which forced it to divide. After that, things took their own course without my part, in accordance with Darwin's theory of evolution."

"That's how I see things too, God. Scientists are already claiming that the formation and division of the first living cell arise from the basic laws of inanimate matter. Soon they will forget to remember you altogether."

"Just let them try!"

"God, if I understand you correctly, after You created the Universe in accordance with all its laws, You no longer influenced the process of evolution in any way.

Tell me, God - can You influence the world of man directly?"

"In what way, for example?"

"Through human consciousness! Could you, for example, prevent a war?"

"No. I couldn't. But I can predict the behaviour of large groups of people on the basis of the Law of Humandynamics. And the prognoses are not at all bad. After all, humanity has left the era of war behind and the time when everyone was against everyone else in the world is now over, people are trying to make war a thing of the past. At least in the part of the world where a greater degree of freedom of choice exists and the price of human life is higher, this goal has already been achieved. Making predictions about the life of a specific individual is however beyond me. Equipped with freedom of choice, people are capable of just about anything! Unfortunately, what they are capable of is not always to the benefit of those around them."

"I have a question for You on a rather sensitive matter. When I meet with any scientific theory, I understand in principle, how the theory was arrived at, how it was developed and what broad experimental data and deep intellectual effort must have been required of its authors. But how Galileo, Newton, Einstein and Darwin made their great discoveries, touching on the very foundations of the Universe is beyond me. These men made real discoveries on a scarce, almost non-existent experimental basis, and no one else who had access to the same data would have dreamed of suggesting the ideas that these few individuals set forth in their theories. Tell me, God, did you give them a hand?"

"Well, how can I put it..."

"Tell me honestly!"

"I shall tell you anyway. But that is enough for today! Wait until next time!"

"No! We have not finished yet! I am just getting started. It's so interesting to talk to You."

"Thank you! Tell me then, human being, what opinion do people have of me?"

"Do you mean, how do they perceive You? I know that you are indifferent to their 'Hosannas and Hallelujahs.' I can tell You how scientists perceive You."

"Yes, that would be very interesting."

"At the dawn of time, people attributed everything to You, good and bad. They praised You for a good harvest and berated You for a bad one. Later, thanks to the divine gift of freedom of choice, particularly observant individuals, who came to be called scientists, began to stand out, and these individuals ordered their observations, drew conclusions and even predicted the occurrence of certain phenomena without making any reference to You at all. Where their knowledge and understanding finished they explained the unknowable as the result of the 'mysterious hand of God.' Gradually, by continuing to make observations and conducting simple experiments, scientists expanded their area of knowledge, and pushed the boundaries of Your influence further and further from the phenomena they were able to explain.

Putting it bluntly, they drew a veil over God and so things continued to the present day. Starting with the Big Bang, scientists explain the origin and development of the entire Universe without involving You, the Creator, at all. There are still some physicists though, who 'refer' to You to explain the difficulties of the zero moment. If you don't mind, God, I'd like to give You an example of my own, that illustrates how people have 'moved You further and further aside' as they have constructed their own picture of the world."

"Why would I mind? I find it interesting!"

"I'd like to tell You about the origin of natural numbers and the very first notion of the Theory of Cognition."

"Are you going to teach me to count?"

"I'm glad you are in a good mood. I am too, but this is a serious topic.

And so, I shall begin by talking only of the natural numbers 1, 2, 3... 'Why?' You may ask. And I would reply that it is because they are directly related to You. In the 19th century, the remarkable German mathematician Leopold Kronecker said: '*God made the integers, all else is the work of man.*' I am going to demonstrate that even here man has done without You."

"Why are you always going out of your way to downgrade my role in the life of man?"

"That is not my intention at all! It simply isn't possible to underestimate Your role in the Universe, God; You created everything, the animate and the inanimate; You gave gene preservation to all living things and to human beings threw freedom of choice into the bargain, which developed in them the powers of observation, the ability to analyse and draw abstract conclusions. And it would seem, that this was enough! I just want to attribute the godly to God and the human to human beings. That's all."

"Carry on then! I'm all ears."

"From the very beginning, primitive humans had to be able to count the objects that surrounded them in the activities of their daily life: people, members of the tribe, domesticated animals, tanned hides for barter, stone tools and finally, their own fingers. They even learned to count the things you cannot touch like the days and nights. Primitive man started by counting homogenous objects: 1 person, 2 people, 3 people... 1 stone, 2 stones, 3 stones... 1 finger, 2 fingers, 3 fingers... etc.

I have no doubt that at first, primitive man perceived the tally for people, the tally for stones and the tally for fingers as different things (never mind the fact that in every cave the numbers 1, 2, 3 and onwards were denoted and named differently), although they may have vaguely suspected that an intimate link existed between objects of a various nature: 1 man - 1 stone - 1 finger... 2 people - 2 stones - 2 fingers... etc. 10 people - 10 stones - 10 fingers - Today mathematicians call this kind of connection *bijection*. But for primitive man, their inklings were not sufficient to comprehend the nature of the connection.

As time went on, life taught primitive man to add homogeneous items, simply by listing them sequentially: 1 man + 1 man = 2 people, 2 peoples + 1 man = 3 people etc. For example, 7 people + 3 people is 10 people. Primitive man learned to use addition in the context of homogeneous objects with animals, stones and of course, fingers.

Then man discovers that the bijective relationship already established between similar quantities of a variety of objects is maintained in the operation of addition, i.e. if 2 people + 3 people = 5 people, then 2 animals + 3 animals will also be equal to 5 animals, just as 2 stones + 3 stones will again equal 5 stones. Mathematicians today refer to the relationship which is maintained in addition as *isomorphism*.

And then it dawned on the primitive mathematician (every cave had their own) that the quality of isomorphism made it possible to count and add objects of a similar nature by replacing their corresponding number and addition with objects of another more convenient nature. For example, if 2 sheep ran into a pen followed by another 3, then if they wanted to know how many sheep were in the pen, there was no need to walk over to the pen themselves and recount the sheep. It was enough to place two fingers of the hand against another three (the first personal computer) and see 5 to be completely confident that there were now exactly 5 sheep in the pen.

Then the primitive mathematician discovers that the bijective relationship is retained not only in the process of addition and subtraction but also in multiplication and division. And then the inevitable happened! Having solved calculations using numbers such as: 1 + 1 = 2, 2 + 1 = 3, etc., the primitive genius finally managed to separate the property of an object from the object itself and created abstract numbers e.g. 1, 2, 3, which later came to be called natural numbers. These numbers are not material objects. Existing in the mind of man, rather than in the natural world, natural numbers enable a person to transfer a tally or arithmetic operation carried out on any type of object to the abstract numbers in the mind, and once a result is achieved, to transfer it back to the original objects.

One can state with confidence that natural numbers were the first abstract mathematical model of the material world. No isomorphism is self-evident. It cannot be proved by logical inference and represents a purely experimental fact.

And although it is tested on a limited number of manipulations with a limited quantity of objects, people nonetheless remain confident of its correctness for objects of any nature and number, just as they remain confident of the validity of other physical laws until such time as they are contravened.

So, what do you think of my little tale?"

"It seems to work."

"But there is no need to be concerned, God. Many people still ardently believe that You are the force that stands behind all phenomena."

"I am not at all concerned! And taking into consideration the fact that I am behind all your 'laws' that explain these phenomena, then perhaps the 'many' are not so mistaken after all?"

"I don't have the knowledge to argue with you, God. So, allow me to take my leave until next time. But let me first remind You, that the two impenetrable secrets of Immanuel Kant, namely the starry sky above and the moral law within us, are today no longer a mystery.

The riddle of the starry sky above has already been solved in detail right down to the first millisecond of the Big Bang itself.

The law of morality within us has also pretty much been cracked. No-one placed this law within us. It simply evolved as a consequence of the clashes that have occurred over thousands and thousands of years between thousands and thousands of individual expressions of free choice."

"Bye for now!"

CONVERSATION 22. THE LAW OF HUMANDYNAMICS AND THE WORLD RELIGIONS.

"God, people use the word religion for everything that is connected with Your name. But even when I was a child it seemed to me that the notions of God and religion were contradictory. There are many religions in the world, but I could not find You in any of them."

"Why do they seem contradictory to you?"

"Because, despite the fact that all world religions have done a lot to unite people within their own sphere of influence, they also have a tendency to lock horns in bloody battle whenever they come into close contact with each other. In the struggle for influence over people's souls, and the exclusive right to represent You on Earth (You who gave life to all living things in the Universe!) the world religions have drawn people into the most brutal and murderous religious wars. And religious conflicts continue to this day. Of course, the real reason for these conflicts is the desire of the religious elite for power and the wealth that power bestows.

Human sacrifice, common in primitive society was also part of the religious practices laid down by the religious hierarchy. How can anyone sanction these things and still speak of God? And that's before you even begin to consider how the majority of priests today live for their own selfish interests. They call for people to live by one set of ethical norms while themselves living by quite a different one. And if that were all, that would surely be bad enough. The Kazakh people have long had to deal with this type of contradiction, advising their children: 'Do as Mullah says, not as he does!'

The main problem is that the ethical instructions which priests give not only inhibit but directly contradict the Laws of Gene Preservation and Freedom of Choice! And yet they claim that the instructions they issue are derived directly from You. Today, representatives of the 'civilised' religions, which are integrated into dictatorial regimes, urge people to embody humility and patience, thereby calling them to reject the divine gift of freedom of choice. They are in effect encouraging people to embrace voluntary slavery in Your name!

And are you aware of what the most honest among them do to themselves in their frantic eagerness to 'serve' You? The Catholic priests, for instance, take a vow of celibacy which clearly contradicts the divine right to gene preservation. Is not the paedophilia that exists among priests a punishment for rejecting Your gift? The giving up of earthly pleasures and ascetic acts of self-denial such as a life spent hungry due to fasting, self-confinement to a monastic cell, hermetic seclusion and even cruel ritualistic flagellation are also practices prevalent among the clergy of many religions.

And aside from that, they like to give children names that mean 'servant of God.' As if that weren't enough they call others to join them in their way of life. God, tell me, is this really what You want? Do You really want slaves? What motivates these people? Do You actually like them?"

"Pride is what motivates them. They strive if only in this manner to gain superiority over others. Those who are close to me are of a different type. They are the ones who live life simply and joyfully; who protect their individual rights to life, i.e. pass on and protect their genes and exercise freedom of choice, and have compassion for the weak in the protection of their rights. I find people interesting who try to understand the animate and inanimate worlds around them, and who in everything seek the ultimate truth, that is, those who try to come as close to me as possible."

"The world religions have undoubtedly played a positive role in softening the heart of man since the very early stages of human society. But I have to say, God, that today the world religions have become hopelessly fossilised, lagging behind secular society, first opposing man's ethical development, and then tardily acknowledging new moral standards that have been adopted without the participation of the church.

The Dalai Lama was forced to admit:

'All the world's religions, with their emphasis on love, compassion, patience, tolerance and forgiveness, can and do promote inner values. But the reality of the world today is that grounding ethics in religion is no longer adequate. This is why I am increasingly convinced that the time has come to find a way of thinking about spirituality and ethics beyond religion altogether.'

And on my own part, I would add: that it is well, that the religions have at least stopped trying to explain the laws of the Universe. I hope You won't be offended, God, if I were to tell you that, according to the authoritative magazine National Geographic[8], belief in You has seriously dropped over the past 10-15 years, most of all in countries which have high levels of freedom of choice."

"Why should I be offended? This is, after all, the result of my own Law of Humandynamics!

---

8 Bullard, Gabe. The World's Newest Major Religion: No Religion. *National Geographic.* [Internet] 22 April 2016. http://news.nationalgeographic.com/2016/04/160422-atheism-agnostic-secular-nones-rising-religion/.

People who seek a life better for their children, who strive to expand their own individual freedom and that of their children, demonstrate faith in me!"

"Thank you! I have one last question to conclude our theme: tell me, God, does the devil really exist? Is the devil Satan, Shaitan, Iblis?"

"And after all our conversations, is this really the question you want to ask me?"

"It's not my question really. My friends are always asking me to put the question to You."

"Why don't you answer them yourself?"

"I cannot bring myself to answer them on Your behalf, God..."

"Then tell me first what would be your answer to them?"

"Well, I don't think that the Devil exists! In fact, I am absolutely certain that there is no such thing. It is just that people, endowed with freedom of choice, like to pass the buck for the evil, underhand and criminal choices they make. They like to be able to blame someone else for pushing them into it. I accept that the things I have done in my life of which I am ashamed of, I have done of my own free will."

"That's a good and honest answer. You can tell your friends, that the Devil is a human contrivance. All evil deeds are committed by people. I know what you think of religion but I wonder what you think of the prophets?"

"Which prophets, in particular, God?"

"The Buddha, Christ, Mohammed."

"I have the greatest respect for them, God. Honestly!"

"Why?"

"They gave everything, even their own lives, to help people to become better human beings."

"And were they successful?"

"Well, the show's not over yet...!"

CONVERSATION 23. HOW MANY COMMANDMENTS, TWO OR TEN? VIRTUE AND SIN. CELEBRATIONS AND PHOBIAS ARISING FROM GENE PRESERVATION AND FREEDOM OF CHOICE. THE LAST FAITH. THE MEANING OF LIFE.

"So God, that brings us to the 'Ten Commandments of God'."

"They aren't my commandments!"

"So whose are they then?"

"Ask Moses."

"I can't ask Moses, as You well know, but that does not matter right now. I would still like us to discuss the Ten Commandments as people usually attribute them to You."

"Ok, then, let's discuss them!"

"Let's begin with the first three:

1. *I am the Lord your God...; You shall have no other gods before me.*

2. *You shall not make for yourself a carved image, or any likeness of anything that is in heaven above, or that is in the earth beneath, or that is in the water under the earth. You shall not bow down to them or serve them, for I the Lord your God am a jealous God, visiting the iniquity of the fathers on the children to the third and the fourth generation of those who hate me, but showing steadfast love to thousands of those who love me and keep my commandments.*

3. *You shall not take the name of the Lord your God in vain, for the Lord will not hold him guiltless who takes his name in vain.*[9]

---

9 Holy Bible: English Standard Version (ESV) Anglicised Edition. Collins (12 April 2012). ISBN 0007466021

Tell me honestly, God, are You unsure of Yourself?"

"Don't forget, I did not create these commandments, so I cannot take responsibility for them."

"Ok, so it was not You. Nonetheless, the first few words of the second commandment: '*You shall not make for yourself a carved image*', considered independently, are particularly interesting and I'd like to come back to them later. Now for the next commandment:

4. *Remember the Sabbath day, to keep it holy. Six days you shall labour, and do all your work, but the seventh day is a Sabbath to the Lord your God. On it you shall not do any work, you, or your son, or your daughter, your male servant, or your female servant, or your livestock, or the sojourner who is within your gates. For in six days the Lord made heaven and earth, the sea, and all that is in them, and rested on the seventh day. Therefore the Lord blessed the Sabbath day and made it holy.*[10]

I suspect this commandment is purely 'technical' in nature and does not require any particular interpretation. No matter how hard people work for their living, even a person who works tirelessly, must occasionally stop to rest, chat with their loved ones, and ponder questions such as: where do I originate from?.., where am I going?.., what is the purpose of my life?... It does not necessarily have to be Saturday, and every nation and every individual should be free to choose the day in the week that suits them best.

Next:

5. *Honour your father and your mother, that your days may be long in the land that the Lord your God is giving you.*[11]

---

10 Holy Bible: English Standard Version (ESV) Anglicised Edition. Collins (12 April 2012). ISBN 0007466021

11 Holy Bible: English Standard Version (ESV) Anglicised Edition. Collins (12 April 2012). ISBN 0007466021

People have not always followed this rule, God. Take primitive man for example, who followed the Law of Gene Preservation blindly. We mentioned at some point ancient legends that have been preserved about primitive societies in which food was extremely scarce. When elderly parents were found to be of no further benefit to the survival of the community, incapable of foraging for food or increasing the number of its members, they would be led into the Valley of Death. With time, as productivity increased, and with it food supplies, and most importantly, with the advent of morality which emerged as an inevitable consequence of the development of freedom of choice, this custom was lost to oblivion and considered nothing more than a barbaric harbinger of the ancient past."

"Why do you think Moses added the words: '*that your days may be long in the land*'?"

"I would have thought You would know the answer to that question better than I, God, but I shall answer you anyway. It's simple. Parents hope that if their children see them caring for their own parents, their children will do likewise and take care of them in their old age, prolonging their time on Earth. This type of behaviour among animals is called 'parenting by example'."

"I enjoyed that explanation. So, what is the next commandment?"

"Next come the most interesting commandments. In turn then:

6. *You shall not murder.*[12]

Old Testament scholars tend to specify the interpretation of this moral principle as 'don't kill without good reason', and I would add: 'either man or beast.' No-one could argue with that. The person

12 Holy Bible: English Standard Version (ESV) Anglicised Edition. Collins (12 April 2012). ISBN 0007466021

who has provided the most general, exacting and universal interpretation of this commandment and, as a result, made it practically unrealisable is Christ himself: 'You shall not kill.' Nonetheless, people have killed both before and after the commandment was given, and in Jesus' name too. Since primitive times, man has had many reasons to kill: to steal a warm cave or food that he may give it to his children, to expand his hunting grounds, to take another's partner (female or male), to continue his own kind, etc. In other words, man has always blindly followed the Law of Gene Preservation. The influence of morality and productivity of labour, which developed from freedom of choice, may help people to control their harsh primal instincts today, but mankind will never be free of them entirely."

"Why not?"

"Because if in exercising their right to gene preservation, one person creates an excessive monopoly on vital resources, the other person has a right to protect their own right to gene preservation by any means because this is Your gift to everyone, the birthright of every single human being."

"I agree with you but you still have not clearly explained what you think about this commandment. So, let me put it differently: are there circumstances under which a person is justified in killing another?"

"I did express my position on this actually. I said that man may protect his right to gene preservation by any means even if that means taking measures to protect his own life or the life of his family. People have exercised this right, like all other living creatures on Earth, throughout human history, without feeling the need to ask anyone else's permission. When a person's right to gene preservation is placed at grave risk by kings, governments and invaders, they will rise up in revolution or go to war to defend this, their basic right. If you like, I could say: 'to defend Your gift to man!' And they will do so without asking You or anyone else, and without fear of killing or being killed."

"Thank you, what flattering recognition. So, tell me, is protecting one's right to gene preservation the only circumstance under which people will overcome the fear of death, rise up in revolution and readily go to war?"

"No, it's not the only reason. There is a second, although it does not relate to everyone. There is a certain portion of the population which emerged by virtue of the fact that Your second gift, freedom of choice, was protected, and although this portion was fairly nominal in primitive society, slowly but surely it has grown over time along with freedom of choice itself. As we have seen throughout human history, people who truly embody freedom of choice will overcome all fear, rise up in revolution and go to war in the name of the gifts You have bestowed upon man, to protect freedom of choice as well as the right to gene preservation."

"Do you think people will always be so cruel, willing to kill others who are like them?"

"No, I don't think so and insurance of that is the Law of Humandynamics. The freer a man is, the more he reveres the freedom of others and the more deeply he understands that any killing is directed against You, and against the divine Law of Gene Preservation. They understand that those who have lost their lives at the hands of another whilst they are still unmarried are deprived of giving birth to the children they would have had, and parents who lose their lives at the hands of another are deprived of the chance of raising their children to adulthood. When a person is killed, their individual freedom of choice, Your divine gift to mankind, is also annihilated.

Only personal freedom can assure observation of the commandment 'You shall not murder'!"

"Do you think that people are always aware of the severity of this sin - murder?"

"I think so, yes. Although in a way, there is murder and then there's murder. Let me share an observation with You.

My childhood took place in the post-war years, the years after the Second World War, among the veterans who had returned from four years spent living in a bloody meat grinder. They had returned from the worst kind of blood-drenched hell ever witnessed in human history. Nonetheless, these men, aside from being heavily shell-shocked, were mentally and morally healthy. They were calm, friendly, always dignified, although, for the most part, the war had left them invalids. They were always very kind to us children.

Why is it then, that so many of the war veterans who returned from Vietnam, Afghanistan and Chechnya were psychologically damaged and in desperate need of rehabilitation? Why aren't they proud of their exploits? Why don't we see them proudly wearing the medals they so deserve?

The answer is simple. The veterans of the Second World War knew without any doubt, that when they fought the Nazis, they were defending their right to gene preservation and even defending their right to the tiny bit of freedom, which the Stalinist regime had left them, which was still more than they could expect to be granted if Hitler were victorious. For these veterans, there was never any doubt that they were fighting for a righteous cause. Conversely, veterans of the Vietnam, Afghan and Chechen wars knew, or at least felt, that their participation in no way protected either their right to gene preservation or their right to freedom of choice. It was not their war. They weren't volunteers. That is why the veterans of these conflicts experienced such grave psychological problems on their return.

Over history, humanity has shed a whole sea of blood, and yet man experiences a kind of natural aversion to war and has always sought to build a society in which there is no need to resort to bloodshed. It is only the development of freedom of choice and the acknowledgement of the human right to freedom of choice among the majority of the population that has allowed man to achieve peace today in the countries of Western Democracy. In this area of the world, one free generation gives birth to another which raises another free generation. We have already said that the level of freedom of choice in these countries is subject to fluctuation, but that does not stop the overall stable tendency towards greater freedom of choice."

"Well ... Once again it is devilishly good to hear that my hopes and efforts related to freedom of choice have not been in vain. Thank you. Only I didn't quite mean to put it like that!"

"Don't worry, God, we are alone. Everyone else is asleep. And there is still a long way to go before dawn. Shall we continue?"

"Go on then, as the others are all asleep..."

"The next commandment is also quite interesting:

7. *You shall not commit adultery.*[13]

Although this commandment is given no further elucidation in the Old Testament, almost all biblical scholars agree that it refers to sexual relations between individuals who are married but

---

13 Holy Bible: English Standard Version (ESV) Anglicised Edition. Collins (12 April 2012). ISBN 0007466021

not each other's spouse. I can understand why this commandment arose: it comes from the fear of receiving a foreign gene
into the family, and of losing one's genes to another family.
This leads to jealousy, which has the same roots as envy, which
we have already discussed on several occasions. Of course, this
commandment, like the others, has played a positive role in the
creation and preservation of the family, and with it, the entire
human race."

"Why is it then, that neither the sixth nor the seventh commandments are observed, especially in the interpretation they
were given by the prophet Christ?"

"It is because, in the attempt to provide as universal and expan-
sive an interpretation of the commandments as possible, Christ
took them to the extreme, even to the point of absurdity, and this
not only led to their rejection but generated the opposite effect
to what was intended. He also threatens retribution for even the
slightest deviation. People aren't keen on being threatened! Look
at what Christ says about the sixth commandment:

> '*You have heard that it was said to those of old, 'You shall not
> murder; and whoever murders will be liable to judgment.' But
> I say to you that everyone who is angry with his brother will be
> liable to judgment; whoever insults his brother will be liable to
> the council; and whoever says, 'You fool!' will be liable to the
> hell of fire.*'[14]

Now listen to his interpretation of the seventh commandment:

> '*You have heard that it was said, 'You shall not commit adul-
> tery.' But I say to you that everyone who looks at a woman*

---

14 Holy Bible: English Standard Version (ESV) Anglicised Edition. Collins (12 April
2012). ISBN 0007466021

with lustful intent has already committed adultery with her in his heart.'[15]

Tell me, God, would You have reasoned in this manner? How exactly are we supposed to look at a woman? How is the human race to continue? How are we to fulfil the Law of Gene Preservation? You're not saying anything. Well, I make my point!

Do you know, God, why this commandment is disregarded most frequently in the West? It is because, as we have said already, the West has the highest levels of freedom of choice. Men and women cannot help but be drawn to the many other attractive individuals they meet, who differ in some way from their own partner, just as we are drawn to many things that are unfamiliar to us. Brought up in a society with a minimal number of taboos, people in the West are used to being able to satisfy their curiosity about the world and feel at liberty to exercise freedom of choice when it comes to human relationships.

It is not just curiosity that draws us to the opposite sex. People sometimes relapse into expressing the Law of Gene Preservation in its primitive, polygamous form and this also contributes to the increase in divorce rates and family breakdown with all its damaging consequences for children. Unfortunately, this gives all breed of traditionalist-moralist an excuse to ride the high moral high ground trumpeting at every corner about the demise of the institution of marriage in the West. I think though, that it is in the West, with its acceptance of relatively free sexual relationships, that we see *marriage beginning to acquire a new form, based not so much on sexual fidelity, as on a common approach to the upbringing of children, which represents the main goal of any free marriage.*"

---

15 Holy Bible: English Standard Version (ESV) Anglicised Edition. Collins (12 April 2012). ISBN 0007466021

"You must be aware that adultery not only leads to divorce but is the cause of immense personal tragedy in the life of the jilted partner. So I have to ask, how can a person allow themselves to become involved in an extra-marital affair knowing the torment it will cause their partner?"

"My response to that, God, is two-fold.

Firstly, it is not for us to say. It's purely a matter of the freedom of choice of any partner who decides to enter into an affair. It's a question of their personal understanding of freedom of choice. There is nothing You or I can do about that, and the entire history of humanity is witness to the fact.

Secondly, as we have already said, *the suffering experienced by the deceived partner stems from jealousy; from feelings which essentially originate from the deep desire to own the body and even the soul of another; from hostility towards the individual freedom of choice of the other. For these reasons, jealousy should be considered a grave sin!* If we were taught from childhood that jealousy was a sin, we would largely mitigate for ourselves the full force of the blow if it were to befall us in the future. If my explanation of the seventh commandment is sufficient, then let's move on to the next one:

8. *You shall not steal.*[16]

This commandment is perhaps the simplest and easiest to understand and it is indeed essential to man, who is by nature a social animal. When the majority in any community fail to observe this commandment it compromises the individual's ability to accumulate the resources necessary to create and maintain a family and to transfer their resources by inheritance, i.e. in practical terms

---

16 Holy Bible: English Standard Version (ESV) Anglicised Edition. Collins (12 April 2012). ISBN 0007466021

it compromises the continuation of the family line and the fulfilment of the Law of Gene Preservation, and consequently leads to the breakdown of the fabric of society. This is why all organised societies prioritise the creation of various kinds of punitive institution (police, courts, prisons) which can ensure that its members' observe the commandment. When the commandment is broken by high-ranking, power-holding members of society, who are in some countries immune to the hand of the law, the right to rebellion and revolution comes into force. Sooner or later the Law of Humandynamics is triggered and the people's right to gene preservation is restored."

"Where does the right to rebellion and revolution originate?"

"In the rights to gene preservation and freedom of choice, God, which You have granted."

"So, tell me then, does society not infringe on the individual's right to freedom of choice when it punishes theft by imprisonment or death?"

"Naturally, but in this case, society implements its own right to freedom of choice: to fight corruption, to survive, to ensure that the individual can preserve its genes rather than accept the situation as it is and perish. Of course, society always chooses the former as the basic foundation for any other solutions it may pursue.

If we are clear on this commandment then let's move on to the next:

9. *You shall not bear false witness against your neighbour.*"[17]

---

17 Holy Bible: English Standard Version (ESV) Anglicised Edition. Collins (12 April 2012). ISBN 0007466021

"What would you like to say about this commandment?"

"To bear false witness is, of course, a heinous crime. As a result of perjury, an innocent person may go to prison deprived of individual freedom of choice at best, or be executed at worst, forfeiting their life and with it the right to gene preservation. So, there can be no doubt that perjury is a sin! History has shown that the sin of perjury can take possession of entire nations. We have seen examples of this in 20th-century communist Russia and Nazi Germany, and in the Middle Ages, in the Spanish Inquisition and in other countries of Europe. The United States was unable to withstand the same sin in the ominous era of McCarthyism, although the wave of false accusations was not quite as rampant there. The sin of bearing false witness is closely connected to another equally grievous sin - the rejection of freedom of choice and voluntarily selling of oneself into slavery - something which has taken place en masse amongst the peoples of Russia and Germany in more recent history. As a result, both these nations were severely punished. This was not Your doing was it, God, by any chance?"

"No, it was nothing to do with me! Have you forgotten that I don't intervene in your life? In the periods of history you mention, serious attempts were made to violate the Law of Freedom of Choice and this triggered the Law of Humandynamics. *To deprive one person of freedom of choice is a considerable sin, but to deprive a whole nation of freedom of choice is a great crime and does not go unpunished.*"

"Did you know, God, that people refer to this kind of punishment as divine retribution? Given that You watch over the Law of Humandynamics, like all other laws of the Universe, perhaps they aren't far wrong?"

"Well, if you like to think of it in that way, I have no objection, except that I would not want people to associate me with the idea of punishment..."

"I think that commandment is clear. Let's move onto the next one:

> *10. You shall not covet your neighbour's house; you shall not covet your neighbour's wife, or his male servant, or his female servant, or his ox, or his donkey, or anything that is your neighbour's.*[18]

I find this commandment highly disputable in the general sense that it is given. Let's look at it bit by bit ignoring the part 'you shall not covet your neighbour's wife', as we have clarified that in our comments on adultery. The next point "(you shall not covet your neighbour's) male servant, or his female servant" must be rejected outright as a flagrant attack on the Law of Freedom of Choice, the main law You have given to man. It is not that we must not desire our neighbour's man-servant or maidservant; we must not desire any kind of servant at all!

And I have serious doubts about the section which reads 'you shall not covet your neighbour's house' or 'his ox.' As I have said repeatedly, God, if the powerful members of any society unfairly seize so many 'homes and oxen', that the weaker members of society cannot survive, no commandment nor anything else for that matter will stop them from 'coveting their neighbour's house and oxen.' Whatever happens, under these circumstances, the weak will find their strength and rise up in revolution.

Blessed are the nations which have learned to solve problems like these without resorting to revolution, and thanks to the divine Law

---

18 Holy Bible: English Standard Version (ESV) Anglicised Edition. Collins (12 April 2012). ISBN 0007466021

of Humandynamics all nations are moving in this direction. I almost said: 'blessed be the Lord, God!'

If You asked me how I would change this commandment, and what precisely it is that one should not covet in one's neighbour, I would have responded:

'You shall not covet your neighbour's soul!'

If people abided by this simple principle many unnecessary personal conflicts could be avoided and much suffering spared. I would add also that the sin of breaking this commandment often arises in people who love each other, like a parent who loves their child, or a spouse who loves their partner, because they fall into the trap of believing that their love gives them some kind of right to the soul of their loved one.

Fundamentalist religious ideologies and totalitarian regimes like that of fascism and communism are responsible for the criminal sin of attacking the soul of the masses. I say criminal because these regimes are inherently self-serving. That's all. That is everything I wanted to say about the tenth commandment."

"Ok, we have gone through all the commandments of Moses. So, tell me, why did You bring this topic up? Not purely for the sake of criticising Moses and contradicting his law, surely?"

"No, not to criticise Moses. I could of course answer You with the words of the prophet Christ: *'Do not think that I have come to abolish the Law or the Prophets; I have not come to abolish them but to fulfil them'*, but that would be too simple. On the one hand, the Ten Commandments are so many that most people cannot memorise them. On the other hand, they are too few in number to give a person guidance for all eventualities of life. Impossible as that may be, the commandments should at least include an instruction to look after one's children and do everything possible to help them 'stand on their own two feet.'

The commandments don't even point to the natural human rights which You have bestowed upon us, like the right to life, the right to continue one's bloodline, the right to basic freedoms etc.

And as far as our sins go, matters are even worse. The late churchmen compiled a list of sins from the usual prohibitions in behaviour that parents teach their children: pride, envy, anger, sloth, avarice, gluttony and lust, but do pride, sloth and gluttony really cause harm to anyone other than oneself? Is it really so sinful to experience envy, anger and greed, feelings that are so natural to most people, as long as one is taught to control them? And Adam and Eve were accused of the last in the list of sins: lust, their's being referred to as the original sin. It's interesting, isn't it? How would I be standing before You now if it weren't for their original sin?

What's more, none of the real sins like villainy, slander, treachery, cowardice, and above all, murder are included in this list at all. Even the presence of the sixth commandment, "You shall not murder" barely justifies the omission.

The main problem is not that the Ten Commandments are imperfect. The question that really troubles me is whether Moses, any other individual or even a single group of people are fit to take upon themselves the responsibility of creating a set of commandments that everyone else must follow?

Where does one person, albeit the wisest of men, acquire the right to teach another?

I do of course recognise the enormously positive role that the Ten Commandments have played in supporting humanity's moral development, and I also understand that they have served as a foundation for the constitution and laws of many nations, but nonetheless...?!"

"So what do you propose? People cannot live without rules; they cannot live without relying on a certain person or set of general laws."

"You are right, God, we cannot! If You have bestowed upon man just two laws: the Law of Gene Preservation and the Law of Freedom of Choice, which no one would dispute, then I propose that we rely on these laws! I suggest that there be just two Commandments based on which every individual must find their own solution to any life situation and decide for themselves what is moral and what isn't. Only in this case will the laws by which people live acquire absolute, or if you like, divine status. And it is of no matter that some people would prefer to replace the word 'divine' with the word 'natural.' That does not change the fundamental underlying point! The two commandments would look like this:

First Commandment:

Preserve your genes and don't harm your neighbour's capacity to preserve theirs.

Second Commandment:

Protect your freedom of choice and do not infringe on the freedom of others."

"Is that all?"

"Yes! Look how all known human rights follow from these two commandments:

In order for a person to be able to follow the first commandment, i.e. exercise their right to continue their bloodline, certain natural rights must be legally secured for them, such as the right to life, the right to property, the right to inviolability of the home, the right to create a family, the right to provide one's family with everything necessary for its survival and well-being, the right to protect one's family by any available means, and finally, the right to sex - a right which, prudishly, has not been mentioned in a single human rights list.

For a person to be able to follow the second commandment, other natural rights must be legally secured such as the right to choose one's activities, the right to choose one's profession, the right to freedom of entrepreneurship, the right to choose one's friends, the right to love, the right to choose one's sexual partner, the right to choose one's marriage partner, the right to freedom of political and religious convictions, the right to form and follow them without harming the rights of others, the right to freely elect and be elected, the right to freedom of movement, and the right to freely choose one's place of residence, the right to freedom of speech, and where freedom of speech is under threat, the right to revolution, etc. Any antitrust law, whether in politics or in the economy, is a law designed to guarantee freedom of choice!

A complete list of essential human rights arising from the commandments of gene preservation and freedom of choice is a matter for lawyers, and would certainly present a broad and interesting field of activity. I hope, God, that You have noted and appreciate the fact, that whereas You only gave man freedom of choice all the other freedoms that result from it human beings have identified for themselves!"

"Yes, I have noticed that and appreciate it, human being you!"

"As You can see, God, none of the ideas I have expressed here are my own. They all follow from Your two fundamental laws, so my suggestion is all honest and straightforward."

"Yes, I agree. So what would you call virtue and what would you call sin?"

"Ah! That's easy. The act of observing the two commandments would be called virtue, and the violation of the commandments, namely the violation of the prohibitions 'do no harm' and 'do not infringe,' would be called sin. All known sins would follow in one way or another from breaking these two commandments."

"For instance?"

"For instance, murder, which is already included in the Ten Commandments, would be the greatest sin against the first 'new commandment.' Today this is considered the most grievous of all sins among all nations but that has not always been the case. Here's another example that follows from the second 'new commandment.' Why does the prophet Moses warn us not to create idols? Why is it that the main Muslim shahada: *'There is no God but God alone, and Muhammad is the messenger of God'*, which goes right back to the days of the prophet, so strongly emphasises that Muhammad is not God, but a prophet of God? Both Moses and Muhammad were well aware that when a person creates an earthly idol, whether it be a leader, a prophet, or anyone else, they give their soul away to that idol. In other words, they give away their Freedom of Choice and as a result, are no longer able to protect it. The prophets called man to follow God and God alone, who is to be found in the heart of every believer.

And the commandment of Christ *'judge not, that you be not judged'*, is this not a way of cautioning people to avoid infringing on the freedom of choice of another? As You can see, God, I still have not added anything new. These are not my own ideas. Quite simply, the time has clearly come to 'gather the stones.' If you look at human history, you can see the ever increasing role of the second commandment. It is not surprising that the main slogan of the Ukrainian protesters at Maidan was: '*Немає гріха важче, як продаж волі своєї*', 'there is no sin greater than selling your own will'."

"You know, 'do not harm' and 'do not infringe' could be understood differently by different people, don't you think?"

"Well, not differently as such, but they could be understood to differing degrees, depending on the level of soul development and personal freedom of each individual. You said yourself God that you gave man freedom of choice so that people would solve the problems of choice themselves rather than turn to you at every step."

"Yes, I did say that but, nonetheless, people still exercise their freedom of choice very little and are quite reticent in doing so."

"You're telling me! In places where the majority has learned to use freedom of choice, people are more tolerant and do genuinely try not to hurt each other, not to influence others and not to limit their freedom. In places where the level of freedom of choice is very low, people are unable to trust themselves and so are still inclined to rely on their leaders, each time getting burned, being disappointed and then forced to engage in bloody conflict. If everything that I have said is clear to You, God, then I'd like to conclude. I would like to call this new system of two commandments the Last Faith."

"Why the last?"

"It is difficult for me to put into words, but I know that for me, this is the last faith I shall come to. The path of my entire life has lead me to this point."

"Ok. So let it be the Last Faith then. Aren't You concerned that with time, people will try and turn it into a religion?"

"I am concerned, but I really hope that won't happen."

"Why?"

"Because all known religions dictate a path by which people must live.

The Last Faith is about the need for people to choose their own path, every day of their life.

And one more thing. As I have already told you, God, the more enlightened people become, the more they embody the gift of freedom of choice which You have given them, and paradoxically, the less they believe in You."

"It's not actually a paradox! I don't believe in anyone either!" What about you though, do you believe in me?"

"I don't know, God. When I talk to you at night, as we are doing now, then I do believe in You, but when I wake up in the mornings, my belief is not as strong because I cannot find a single material fact of Your existence, and so I wait the next night with great impatience. Let's go on talking about the commandments. God, is it alright for me to pass these Old-New Commandments on to other people?"

"Yes, you have a responsibility to pass them on!"

"And can I lie, God, and tell them that these are Your Commandments?"

"Yes, why not? That is what all the prophets have done."

"I appreciate the mention as a prophet, even if you are being ironic. What is it that you don't like about the prophets?"

"What makes you think I don't like them? All the prophets were sincere in their compassion for other people, for my creations, and each in their own way wanted to help the rest of humanity with whatever each prophet saw as the main cause of human suffering: one jumped from here and ran to people with fire, so they could be warm; another scratched something on to some stones, and making me sign a text I had barely read, took it to the people insisting that now they would know how to live in the right way; the third brought them comfort and belief in life after death, and the fourth something else... There have been so many of you, I can't remember them all. The question is, what will *your* two Commandments give people?"

"I want to give people self-confidence, confidence in their inner freedom."

"And in what might they have confidence? In the 'bright future of all humanity' as your communist-fathers once taught?"

"You can be sarcastic if You like, but people really do need that kind of certainty."

"Why do they?"

"Because all religions and moral codes that have been invented so far have always reproached people for not leading the right kind of life and demanded that they observe behavioural norms they are not strong enough to follow. People are always expected to live with it and submit to force, but then they rise up in Revolution and go to war when a real threat looms over their natural right to gene preservation and freedom of choice. Both individually and as groups, people have instinctively, often subconsciously, followed these two commandments in all their activities and strivings.

I assert that *in spite of our many mistakes, throughout human history people have lived in the right way and continue to live in the right way!*

And the proof of this assertion is the Law of Humandynamics and the very fact of the huge growth of freedom of choice in the world. Once people understand this, they will finally acquire some self-confidence!"

"What for?"

"Lack of confidence in one's personal righteousness, lack of inner freedom is the main source of spiritual confusion and un-happiness that people suffer in their lives today and this is the case even in democratic, prosperous countries where putting food on the table and a roof over one's head is no longer a problem.

Man cannot live without man, but living with man is not easy either.

People have not everywhere learned to respect the personal free-doms of others. And whereas a person knows what to do when their personal freedom of choice is under external threat, they are usu-ally totally lost when the threat comes from the people to whom they are closest. You often hear parents telling their children that they are not as nice as all the other children. A wife will criticise her husband for not being the ideal she always dreamed of (or a hus-band criticises his wife in the same way). And when they reach ado-lescence, it is the children's turn and they criticise their parents.

In totalitarian countries, people fall victim to mass criticism for not being sufficiently patriotic by state institutions who invent idols the public are obliged to worship. All that criticism makes it very difficult for the individual to feel emotionally comfortable.

You might ask whether criteria exist based upon which the individual can protect their inner world, the 'self?' In this regard, I recall a story about a small-town Jewish rabbi called Zusya, who said that when he finally appears before You, You won't ask him: 'Zusya, why weren't you like Abraham or Moses?', you'll ask him: 'Zusya, why weren't you like Zusya?'

Have you ever heard of Zusya, God?"

"No, I haven't, but your Zusya was quite right! I don't need a thousand Abrahams or a thousand Moses. I gave freedom of choice to each person individually, so that they could exercise personal freedom as they saw fit. So tell me, what do *you* want to give people?"

"Freedom!"

"What?"

"I want to convey to every individual that they have a God-given right to freedom of choice!"

"That's better! Continue!"

"And I want to strengthen those who have been deprived of this right, in their battle for Your gift. And I want to remind those who have forgotten this divine right is also theirs."

"You do know that *freedom of itself never guaranteed anyone happiness?*"

"Yes, I do and I also know, that *without freedom no happiness is possible at all,* neither happiness, hope nor personal development.

Without freedom, people will never acquire a feeling of self-confidence."

"Is everyone lacking in self-confidence?"

"No, not everyone. Only the weak, but the majority are weak. People who are strong in their faith find support in their religion and acquire an inner strength but the number of people who believe in the traditional religions is falling because they no longer seem to offer answers to the questions that most concern us.

Where faith in You is blind or non-existent this situation is abused by all sorts of pastor-like villains who only serve to turn one group of people against another, sowing death and annihilating efforts to fulfil the Law of Gene Preservation. They usurp the thoughts and souls of the innocent, contravening the Law of Freedom of Choice.

I want people who observe these two simple commandments to be confident that they are living righteously!

As far as possible, I want to free people from painful and unnecessary doubt and bring them closer to You."

"For what purpose? Do you think I am free of all doubt?"

"No, not necessarily. But I would like human doubts to be more like the doubts You experience. I want people to live almost like the gods do, like You do."

"You display a great deal of pride you know, and you will pass your pride on to others, but what else could one expect from someone who lives only for freedom of choice?"

"Feci quod potui, faciant meliora potentes!"[19]

---

19 I have done what I could; let those who can do better!

"Then let's..."

"Wait, God, don't go yet... I have one last question."

"Ok, Go ahead and ask!"

"What is the meaning of life?"

"Don't you know?"

"No."

"I don't know either."

"How can You not know?! Why then did You take up with life in the first place?"

"If I had the answer to this question, and one that would suit everyone, I would have manifested the response long ago and with that, have been done with this life. What about you? Do you have any thoughts on the subject?"

"Yes, some. I am certain that there is no singular meaning of life that applies equally to everyone. If you look at the prophets of whom we were talking earlier, you can see that each interpreted the meaning of life differently. It reminds me of the parable of the six great Jewish prophets. In answer to the question: 'where is truth?', the meaning of life, the first Prophet, Moses, 'who had revealed' the one God to the people, pointed a finger up towards the sky; the second prophet, Solomon, who was known for his great wisdom, pointed a finger to his head; the third prophet, Jesus Christ, who had called the world to compassion placed his hand on his heart; the fourth prophet, Karl Marx, who led the class struggle and the battle for survival, stroked his stomach; the fifth prophet, Sigmund Freud, with his basic instinct pointed, naturally, a little lower. Then came the sixth prophet, Albert Einstein, who declared that the answer to the question was relative and depended on a system of coordinates specific to the person concerned. So you see, God, not even the prophets had a uniform interpretation of the meaning of life.

And so with regard to what we, Homo Vulgaris, are to do, I can only answer for myself, based on the Last Faith.

Raise your children and look after your soul every day of your life until the last day when you hand it over to God personally, hopefully, in a more developed form than when you received it.

And with that, goodbye God!"

"Hang on a moment! Now I have some questions of my own."

"Ok, ask me!"

"You said that people live according to the laws of gene preservation and freedom of choice, whether they are aware of it or not. What is the attitude to the laws I have given you? How do people relate to the Law of Gene Preservation for example?"

"People are very positive about it, God! Like all living beings, we try to follow it, as far as we are able. Men love women and women, men..."

"That is not quite what I meant. What is the emotional response to these laws?"

"It's very positive. Weddings are hugely celebrated as a laying of the foundations for the fulfilment of the Law of Gene Preservation and then, nine months later, the consequence of the fulfilment of the law, the birth of a child, is no less cause for general celebration. We celebrate this date joyfully every year. Weddings and birthdays are our most important festivals. What are they if not celebrations of the Law of Gene Preservation?! So, God, you can rest assured!

In contrast to the Law of Gene Preservation, I cannot say that people follow the Law of Freedom of Choice with the same confidence or in the same numbers. The thing is that one person's attempt to use your gift of freedom of choice, often clashes instantly with the free choice of other members of society, in most cases more powerful than themselves, and this naturally evokes a certain amount of fear. As You said yourself, God, the Law of Freedom of Choice is relatively recent and *so a large part of the world has still not achieved the general balance of liberty for all individual members and segments of society that we call democracy. Eventually, though, all nations will arrive at democracy because the Law of Humandynamics will leave them no other path to follow.*

Having said that, as far as they are able, every individual follows the Law of Freedom of Choice, whether they are consciously aware of it or not. They instinctively strive to extend the scope of freedom of choice both for themselves and for their children. Don't good schooling and a decent university education give a person greater freedom of choice, just as winning a competition, contest, gaining a promotion, an increase in salary, or developing one's personal business do? This is why people celebrate so joyfully every step on their path through life with their friends and family. What are these events if not celebrations of the Law of Freedom of Choice?! Many peoples celebrate national holidays that mark the dates of revolutions that have won them independence or brought them democracy. In other words, events that have given them greater degrees of freedom. The desire for wealth is also an intuitive striving for greater personal freedom. Yet without consistent work on behalf of the soul, the 'freedom of choice' that wealth brings will remain an illusion. After satisfying the flesh, a weak soul is left with no choice at all.

As You can see, God, we human beings see the Law of Freedom of Choice as an expression of Your grace. I would add that all our human fears and phobias are also related to these two laws. The fear of losing a child, of infertility and impotence are all basically, the fear of losing the right to gene preservation. Fear of losing one's job, of becoming ill, losing one's independence, financial ruin, imprisonment - these are all fundamentally the same fear of losing freedom of choice. When you really look at it, all our sorrows and troubles are related to some kind of infringement or the actual loss of these two sacred rights."

"Ok. So are you hoping, that having introduced people to the laws they live by, you will somehow radically change their life?"

"I am not that naive, God. No-one has ever managed that. Even You have repeatedly acknowledged that having created the laws of nature and set them in full motion, You no longer have any influence on their development."

"Yes, that is true. What about the prophets then, who you so revere, claiming that every one of them has altered peoples' lives hugely and over many centuries?"

"I am not belittling the role of the prophets, God, but those who did actually exert a huge influence on history were born at bifurcation points on the arrow of time, along with others, the first individuals who were capable of understanding and accepting their ideas. For example, when Christ appeared with his idea of compassion, freedom of choice had for centuries been preparing the souls of the first few individuals who would be receptive to him. There would have been a very different response if Christ had preached compassion in the caves to the primitive peoples. They would have eaten him alive!

My goal is far more modest. I want people to learn to understand the reasons for their behaviour and the behaviour of others within the context of these two laws so that they can avoid unnecessary conflict. I want people to be confident in the knowledge that *the right to gene preservation and the right to freedom of choice are given to man by You, God - that this is our birthright, something that should not be usurped by anyone else, ever, under any circumstances.*"

"Well, I think we have exhausted that topic for today."

"Goodbye!"

CONVERSATION 24. JESUS AND JUDAS

"Why have You chosen this as the topic of our conversation today?"

"This topic is directly related to The Freedom of Choice. Well, God, a long time ago, back in my student days, when I first read the Gospel, I was left with a strong impression of the 'theatricality' of the narrative especially in the 'Jesus and Judas' story line.

Judas' betrayal, his remorse, repentance, and resulting suicide, are written as if in accordance with the banal conventions of 'poor theatre' and as a result, the entire Gospel plot is totally unconvincing. At least that was my impression.

I read all four gospels again and again, and following a trail left by the evangelists, perhaps inadvertently, I discovered things in the text that only served to confirm my suspicions. Nothing in the behaviour of Judas, the apostle who was closest to the teacher, sets him apart to be any darker in character than the other apostles, and there is nothing in the text to hint at his future betrayal. Most of all I was troubled by Jesus' reply '*You have said so!*' as described by Matthew, when Judas asks '*Is it I, Rabbi (who shall betray You?).*'

Jesus' answer has been interpreted as a prophecy for more than two thousand years and yet in his words I heard something more like a command.

And I even felt that the famous '*kiss of Judas*' was more a sign of farewell than treachery. The evangelists' attempt to portray Judas in a negative light seemed to me quite flimsy: their speculations as to Judas' greed, such as his objections to precious oil being wasted on the anointing of Jesus' feet instead of being sold and the money given to the poor, are all quite unfounded. Judas' objections may equally illustrate that Judas, more than any of the other apostles, had adopted Christ's teaching of compassion for the poor. No one can testify that Judas conspired with the chief priests, unlike so many other events that took place in the presence of large numbers of witnesses. What could be the explanation for why Christ sent Judas so persistently to do what he had to do, something about which only the two of them knew?

Why did Christ, who feared death like anyone else, not make use of the escape routes deliberately left for him in his questioning by Caiaphas and Pontius Pilate?

And finally, would a person capable of committing the most heinous crime in the history of human betrayal really be driven to hang themselves by sudden pangs of conscience? I would hate to think that the attitude towards Judas on behalf of the apostle-evangelists who described these events was simply one of envy and jealousy on account of their Teacher.

I was greatly confused by it all, until one day, I had a wonderful dream. I saw myself in the garden of Gethsemane on the very night the Saviour was arrested and taken to be judged. It was a moonlit night and unseen by anyone I stood beneath the crown of a large olive tree. There I became an involuntary witness to a secret conversation that took place between Jesus and Judas who were standing behind the same tree. Judas was crying, refusing to do what Jesus asked, saying that he and his descendants would be cursed for centuries. Jesus insisted, ardently trying to convince Judas by saying that he could not trust any of the other disciples to carry out the task. I listened spellbound standing so close to Christ that I could have reached out and touched his garments. Then the pair withdrew, continuing to talk quietly as they walked and I could tell from the way Judas's back was slightly sunken that he had resigned himself to the deed.

The next morning, I recounted the dream to my university friends. They were surprised by what I told them, but that was all and I soon happily forgot about the dream entirely. Fifteen years later, as fate would have it, I found myself in North Africa, in Algeria. Standing in an olive grove for the very first time I was struck by the aroma emanating from the olive trees and recognised the same smell that had remained in my memory from the wonderful dream I had once dreamed faraway, in snowy Siberia. Staggered by the connection I returned to the memory of my dream over and over again until I could remember the conversation I had overheard between Jesus and Judas in minute detail. I was left with no doubt that the details of the dream did indeed describe how everything had taken place in real life.

Jesus wrote the scene of his own tragic death, produced it, and played the main part.

I naturally began to ask myself why Christ had to die in the way he did, and why he needed Judas to betray him. Could he not have continued to go from village to village continuing to preach his ideas as he had already been doing, and not without success? What was this, to put it bluntly, PR stunt for? This is the question I wanted to put to You today, God."

"Alright then, I shall try to answer you. I remember that story well, in which, among other things, they also made reference to me. How many followers had already embraced the teachings of Christ at that time? There were just the twelve apostles, plus a dozen or so idle listeners who tagged along behind. Christ's sermons, which hardly helped 'strengthen' the position either of the local Jewish or the Roman authorities, had firmly caught the interest of the security services. You can imagine how preacher-dissidents like Christ usually ended up. That's right! They would be taken out by a secret assassin, or worse, discredited in the eyes of the crowd.

In these circumstances could Christ rely on the widespread propaganda of his views and on the immortality of his great ideas which he valued more than his own life? Of course not! Imagine the world without newspapers, television or the internet! What else could he do? Of course, Jesus was an exultant individual but he definitely was not stupid. He understood very well, that sooner or later Caiaphas' people would have him killed for the sermons he was preaching. It was highly likely that they would kill him secretly, that there would be a 'mysterious disappearance' of his person. Jesus understood that only his 'loud death to the world' would immortalise his name and ideas; only by '*overcoming death by death*', so to speak, could he convey his teaching to the largest number of people. So he decided to write the death scene, which you call 'poor theatre.' Try to understand and forgive!"

"I do understand, God! I understand now and I mourn his great death. Before, I saw Christ as nothing more than a victim of some banal betrayal, but now, thanks to your explanation, I realise that Jesus arranged his own death. Like everyone else, he could have got married and had children and like everyone else, lived only for the sake of earthly pleasures, but he made a different choice. The greatest choice in history. For the sake of humanity. His feat is all the greater for that choice.

I mourn the death of Judas too, who took upon himself the most terrible mission of all the apostles: to be cursed for centuries. May their souls rest in peace, God!"

CONVERSATION 25. JESUS CHRIST: LOVE OR COMPASSION?

"Hello, God! As always, I have some questions I would like to ask You."

"Ok. You have my full attention..."

"In both Testaments of the Bible there are parts I don't understand. I know, God, what You think of the Bible, but there is no-one else I can ask. No theologian has been able to give me an intelligible response to the questions that concern me. You, however, are mentioned in the Bible frequently and so must have witnessed all the events described in the Gospel.

So my first and most important question is this: In the New Testament Christ commands us: '*Love your neighbour as yourself.*' I accept that it is possible to love one's children, one's parents, a lover, friends and relatives. I can even imagine that it is possible to love one's immediate neighbour, but how can you love everyone, as Christ calls us to do? I can only speak for myself but I can't imagine being able to love the whole world, all humanity, as myself. I want to be totally honest with You about these things, God!

The very first time that I read the New Testament I had the feeling that ***Christ experienced great compassion for people, as those who are strong usually feel towards the weak.*** As I continued to read the gospels my sense of Jesus's compassion, which can be easily traced through all four Canonical Gospels, grew much stronger."

"Well, when you arrive here, you can ask Jesus about that yourself."

"You know, God, despite my respect for You, I am in no hurry to return. When my time comes I will be with You and I shall visit

Jesus and speak to him, but it's important to me to know the answer to my question in the here and now."

"Ok. Do you know what language the New Testament was originally written in and from which language it was later translated?"

"Yes, Greek."

"Do you have access to the internet and Google? Look up the Greek words for 'love' and 'compassion'."

"I'll look them up right now... Got it! I should have guessed! In Greek 'love' and 'compassion' are synonyms of the word 'sympathy.' So, does this mean that the first translators of the New Testament made the wrong choice: instead of the meaning 'Sympathy-Compassion' (which nowadays is more often called 'Empathy'), they chose the meaning 'Sympathy-Love'? That explains things. So in this light, the commandment should read differently:

Have compassion for your neighbour, as for yourself

That's quite natural! After all, the beginnings of compassion can be observed even among herd animals. Compassion seems to be an essential element to the survival of the members of the herd. Jesus was evidently the first person, to have a deep understanding of the fact that unless people learned compassion, human society could not survive.

Tell me though, God, why haven't You helped people arrive at the correct understanding of the commandment on compassion before now?"

"You have forgotten again that I live by the principle of non-intervention in human affairs. Have you come across any other difficulties in interpreting the Bible?"

"Yes! God, was Jesus in any respects a politician?"

"In what sense a politician?"

"Did he always say what he thought irrespective of the political situation?"

"Why do you ask?"

"When the Pharisees tried to provoke Jesus by asking him whether the people should pay taxes to Caesar, Jesus replied with the words: *'Render to Caesar the things that are Caesar's, and to God the things that are God's.'* **These words are very well-known today and are oft quoted in various situations of life.** I don't think Jesus was a politician. I am certain that he would have been against the taxes and against the Roman occupation in general. I think he was just conscious of the political situation he found himself in and the people his words were aimed and so gave that answer so that he would not be arrested before he had time to share his overriding plan with others. He stayed loyal to his foremost intention and went to Golgotha totally conscious of what he was doing. What do You make of my interpretation?"

"It has its place. Was there anything else you wanted to ask?"

"Yes, but I think I can deal with that one myself now. Most importantly, I now understand the places in the Gospels that I didn't understand before! Thank you, God. Goodbye!"

"Wait! I now have a question for you."

"Ok, God, ask me!'

"In your eyes, who is Jesus: the son of God or the son of man?"

"Surely You must know the answer to that, God."

"Of course I know, but I wanted to hear your opinion."

"For me, Christ is undoubtedly the son of man!

I have been lucky enough to have met people like him in life."

"Then let us say farewell now, human being!"

"Why farewell, God?"

"Farewell, until our final meeting..."

"What final meeting?"

"The one which no-one can avoid..."

"God, wait, don't go! I need one more meeting with You here on Earth!"

"What for?"

"I want to confess..."

"Are you ready?"

"Yes!"

"Ok. Then let there be one more meeting."

"I shall call this meeting the epilogue..."

"Goodbye!"

Epilogue.
Confession. Forgiveness and Farewell.

"So, God, this is our second to last meeting. I have already asked everything that I wanted to ask You, and have said everything I wanted to say. It is time to bring things to a close. There must be many others besides myself who want to speak with You."

"Hang on a moment! I wanted to know how old you were when you first learned of me?"

"I did not learn about you. I felt You on the day of my father's funeral. You took him back when I was seven. Everyone around me was crying and then I felt someone place a hand on my shoulder and quietly speak the words: 'There is no need to be afraid. I will be with you.' I looked around but there was no-one standing close by. I was left without a father or older brother and had to face the world alone and all that was in it, both good and bad. It seemed so huge and terrifying. Ever since then, every time You led me from one trial of life to another, I knew that You would always come to my aid. When I was still a child, You came in the form of a person who was kind and strong. Later, when I found myself in situations that seemed hopeless, I never fell into despair as I knew that you would show me an unfailing solution to the problem. Later I came to understand that in this way You were showing me the full spectrum of human nature, the highest flight of the human spirit and its descent into the deepest abyss. I experienced all these states at a young age. And so whilst still young, I learned to protect myself and to fear nothing and no-one. Since childhood I have had no fear of authority, government officials or the management at work. I have never understood the general climate of fear in which we live, even taking account of the terror the Communists instilled in my own people that subjected their souls to slavery. I did not fear You, God, either, although I have always respected You."

"What for?"

"For creating what man could not.

If there is something I have feared and still fear today, it is to be indebted, because debt always limits freedom of choice. Once I realised that the great gift to man, freedom of choice, is Your gift and only Yours, I resolved never to trifle with freedom in any circumstances."

"Have you sinned?"

"I don't know God. In what sense do you mean 'sinned'?"

"In the same sense that people usually understand the word."

"Well, God, You already know that for me, a sin is simply a departure from the two commandments of the Last Faith. I have not departed from them and nonetheless, I shall answer You in the manner according to which people usually understand the word sin.

Of course, I was no example for the young: I started smoking very early, liked to drink with my friends, got into fights with them 'wall to wall', but I never betrayed anyone. I never stole; I have never given false witness, and have never bowed my head before anyone. I have never broken an oath because I have never sworn any, even in the child and youth organisations of the communist regime, in which I grew up, where taking oaths was compulsory. I never made vows at the marriage altar. I have never sworn allegiance to anyone or anything because any oath, any allegiance, tethers Your gift of freedom of choice. I have never abandoned anyone in trouble, neither man nor animal.

The only thing is, perhaps, that I have always loved beautiful women. A lot..."

"That's not a sin. That's simply *conscious freedom of choice with the unconscious desire to pass on and protect your genes*."

"Well done! Very nicely put! I could not have put it better myself!"

"Are you really praising me?"

"Yes, sorry God, I am just full of admiration! Let's continue. Listen to me! You'd think I was totally spotless. That is not how others would see me."

"You're only free of sin within your own value system of sins and virtues. Perhaps, that is enough for you. What else did you want to say?"

"I really wanted to thank You, God, for the life that You have given me. For all the hardships and losses, for all the fortuitous gains that led me to the Last Faith. For never abandoning me, for always giving me strength of spirit in difficult moments and never forcing me to go against my heart.

Thank you for the friends You have given me. They were all so clever and such honourable souls. From them, I have learned what it means to stand shoulder to shoulder with a friend in battle. The best years of my life were spent with them. They were unrivalled, untethered in their awareness of personal freedom of choice and so many of them have returned to You before their time. You gave them to be born free in the unfree country. They walked their path in life, as by the testament of Jesus according to Matthew, through 'the narrow gate.' And having known people like them, I can no longer socialise or even sit at the same table with those who have voluntarily chosen the path of the slave. Sorry, God!

Thank you for the women You have given me - beautiful and loyal. I was happy, with all of them. Forgive me, God, that I was unable to make them happy."

"A free person can never give anyone else happiness, except perhaps to teach them freedom..."

"Thank you, God, for everything. *Thank you for the crashing waves of the ocean, for the pre-dawn stillness of the lake, for the African sunset, for the ray of sunlight streaming through the leaves, for the path of moonlight on the night sea, for the spring breeze blowing on my face, for the smell of the sea, for the farewell call of a swan in the autumn sky and for the child's first laugh. It is in these moments that I have felt the sharp feeling of your invisible but tangible presence.* Thank you!"

"Is there anything you want to ask me for?"

"You know me, God, I have never asked You for anything. But there is something I shall ask for now. My parents are both with You. Look after them."

"Is there anything else?"

"Make sure the souls of my friends rest in peace, those who are already with You. They suffered in life because life is hard for people who are master of their own choices, whose souls are restless, constantly held in a condition of having to choose. And receive with Your grace the restless souls of those who are still here when their hour comes."

"And what about your own soul?"

"She is at peace, God. My soul has been at peace since I embraced the Last Faith. I am no longer tormented by the doubts that have plagued me in my life. My soul has found peace, here on Earth."

"Is there anything you regret?"

"No! I don't regret anything. What regrets can a person have who has spent their entire life doing everything of their own free will, according to their own freedom of choice? And anyway, to regret the past is like regretting the fact that time only passes in one direction."

"Who do you want to spend time with when you return to me?"

"So, does that mean there's freedom of choice there with You too?"

"Yes, why not? Where else would it be, if not here? I remember when one of your prophets, Mahatma Gandhi died. Of course, we did not delay him in purgatory and let him in straight away. I did not even have time to ask him with whom he wished to spend his time here. He rushed past me, barely glancing in my direction and made straight for Leo Tolstoy:

> *'Mr. Tolstoy, I am so happy to see you' he said. 'I've been dreaming of being able to talk with you for such a long time! We corresponded when we were on Earth. Do you remember?'*

> *'Hello, hello, dear Mohandas!', said Tolstoy. 'Of course, I remember! I have not had such good luck. I have spent years waiting to meet Ecclesiast and have just this minute been granted an audience. What can be done? You know what, let's go together! I'll tell Ecclesiast that you're with me.'*

So I shall ask you again. 'Who do you want to spend time with when you return to me'?"

"With the friends from my youth!"

"Ok. Goodbye for now then."

"Yes, until we meet again, for the last time…"